WORLD HISTORY

THE BIG ERAS

A Compact History of Humankind for Teachers and Students

A Companion to World History for Us All
A Model Curriculum for World History
http://worldhistoryforusall.sdsu.edu

Edmund Burke III
Research Professor of History
University of California, Santa Cruz

David Christian
Professor of History
Macquarie University, Sydney
Institute for World and Global History
Ewha Womans University, Seoul

Ross E. Dunn
Professor Emeritus of History
San Diego State University

   NATIONAL CENTER FOR HISTORY IN THE SCHOOLS, UCLA

©2012 The Regents, University of California

Published by
Social Studies School Service
10200 Jefferson Boulevard, P.O. Box 802
Culver City, CA 90232-0802
United States of America

(310) 839-2436
(800) 421-4246

Fax: (800) 944-5432
Fax: (310) 839-2249

www.socialstudies.com
access@socialstudies.com

ISBN: 978-1-56004-764-3

Product Code: Z213

TABLE OF CONTENTS

PREFACE

World History: The Big Eras is a very short history of the world written to encourage teachers and students to think about the human past on a big scale. It brings together the essays that introduce the nine Big Eras in World History for Us All, a web-based model curriculum for world history available online at http://worldhistoryforusall.sdsu.edu. These Big Eras constitute the periodization plan and the basic organizational structure of the World History for Us All curriculum. Many teachers have requested a printed compilation of the Big Era essays to help guide them and their students in exploring historical developments, continuities, and turning points on a larger scale than textbooks or content standards lists offer.

This little book is an interpretive narrative of the human past from the origins of the universe to today. The nine chapters are identical to revised versions of the nine Big Era introductory essays in World History for Us All. Each of these essays is organized in three primary sections: Humans and the Environment, Humans and Other Humans, and Humans and Ideas. These three headings correspond to the thematic component of World History for Us All called the Three Essential Questions. Teachers and students may refer to the website for ways to use the Three Essential Questions in classrooms. The book's Introduction includes text drawn from the "History, Geography, and Time" section of the online model curriculum. The Epilogue corresponds to the section titled "Reflecting on the Past, Thinking about the Future."

Educators may use this book as a companion to World History for Us All online or as an independent resource in any world history course. This book aims to serve both instructors and students in exploring historical vistas on the scale of continents, hemispheres, ocean basins, and the globe as a whole—a perspective that detailed, civilization-by-civilization textbooks usually do not provide. Teachers grappling with coverage of state and district history and social science standards will find this narrative useful in connecting specific content topics to wider historical landscapes. The global approach taken here is also highly compatible with the Advanced Placement World History course, which focuses on "big ideas of continuity and change." Finally, we believe this book offers instructors and students in college and university world history courses a panoramic frame for investigating the past at a variety of scales of time and space.

Each chapter includes optional study questions that may be used for classroom discussions, homework, or essay assignments.

This book and the World History for Us All model curriculum use the secular designations BCE (Before the Common Era) and CE (Common Era) in place of BC and AD. This usage follows the format of the National Standards for History and the Advanced Placement World History course. It in no way alters the conventional Gregorian calendar. We also use BP (Before Present) for historical periods approximately prior to 10,000 BP.

Edmund Burke III
David Christian
Ross E. Dunn

ACKNOWLEDGMENTS

World History: The Big Eras is just one of the fruits of the web-based World History for Us All model curriculum project that, since 2001, has involved several dozen teachers, scholars, technology experts, and graphic designers. In one way or another, directly or indirectly, all of these professionals have contributed to the development of this book. We are especially indebted to the educators and scholars who laid the conceptual and intellectual foundations of World History for Us All during three successive summer workshops at San Diego State University:

Simone Arias	Felicia Eppley
Bob Bain	Bill Foreman
Mary Bickley	Donald Johnson
Avi Black	Jean Johnson
Bill Bravman	Ernest O'Roark
Anne Chapman	Ellen Leader Pike
Sharon Cohen	Irene Segade
Susan Douglass	Eileen Wood

We invite readers to refer to the web site (http://worldhistoryforusall.sdsu.edu) for a full listing of project participants.

We would like to thank the Ahmanson Foundation for three generous grants in support of World History for Us All, including funding specifically designated for this book's development. Other supporters since the project's inception have included the National Endowment for the Humanities; the Longview Foundation; the National Center for History in the Schools (NCHS) at the University of California, Los Angeles; and San Diego State University's President's Leadership Fund and College of Arts and Letters.

We would like to thank Ingrid de Haas, the project's content manager, for her sharp editing skills. Marian Olivas, the Program Coordinator of the NCHS, helped guide this book's final production stages and has otherwise dedicated herself to World History for Us All in numerous ways. This volume has also much benefitted from the advice and collaboration of Gary B. Nash, Director of the NCHS. We thank Anne Chapman, a long-time member of the NCHS team, for developing the chapter study questions. All maps in Chapters 1–9 were designed by Gareth Mann. To see more historical maps by him, visit www.MapsofWorldHistory.com.

Finally, World History for Us All has enjoyed the continuing moral and material support of both the NCHS network of history educators and San Diego State University, especially its History Department.

History, Geography, and Time

Today, world history is a basic subject in the social studies curriculum across the United States. K–12 educators generally agree that young Americans graduating from high school should have knowledge of world history, geography, and contemporary affairs. A world history education should include the whole world and not just part of it. The subject is challenging, however, because it embraces humanity in general, not just one nation or cultural tradition, and because the time scope—from the Paleolithic era to the present—is immense.

Getting the whole world into world history does not mean that students must investigate "everything," and certainly not everything all at once! To make sense of the past, we have to organize the investigation into manageable pieces. We must define specific historical topics, questions, problems, time periods, and themes, then explore them in careful ways. Students, however, should not lose sight of the main subject: the story of how humans have behaved, thought, and interacted across the ages.

In this book, each of the Big Era chapters addresses a time period on the global scale. Each successive Big Era is shorter in time scope than the previous one. For example,

Dual Research Base of World History for Us All

Scholarship on World History

Scholarship on Teaching and Learning History

Big Era One considers the very long epoch of history up to the emergence of Homo sapiens. Big Era Nine, by contrast, focuses on the period from 1945 to the present. This approach is generally compatible with conventional organization of courses, standards, and textbooks. It also mirrors the long-term trend of historical change: human interrelations have become increasingly complex, and the speed of change has continuously accelerated. Consequently, recent Big Eras should encompass shorter time periods than more distant ones if investigation of them is to be coherent and intelligible.

This book and the World History for Us All model curriculum generally have a dual research base. One is the exciting research in comparative, interregional, and world-scale history that scholars have undertaken during the past several decades. This scholarship has shown that although nation-states and civilizations are appropriate contexts for studying historical change, other configurations of space and time are valid as well. Patrick Manning has argued that the central aim of world history is to investigate "the interaction of the pieces (be they community, societal, or continental) in human history" and "to assess the experience of the whole of humanity through study of those interactions."[1] World history also involves searches for answers to questions about the past that may lead the searcher straight across the boundaries of nations, empires, and civilizations. World History for Us All has adopted the premise that when teachers and students pose good historical questions, even very big questions, they can explore answers in ways that charge their study with historical meaning and contemporary relevance. As historian David Christian writes:

> In a world with nuclear weapons and ecological problems that cross all national borders, we desperately need to see humanity as a whole. Accounts of the past that focus primarily on the divisions between nations, religions, and cultures are beginning to look parochial and anachronistic—even dangerous. So, it is not true that history becomes vacuous at large scales. Familiar objects may vanish, but new and important objects and problems come into view.[2]

The other part of the World History for Us All research base is the work that scholars in the United States, Britain, and other countries have done on the ways students learn, interpret, and understand the past. They have been asking, "How do students build meaning from historical information, and how do they connect facts to broader patterns and generalizations?" These writers argue that historical understanding requires learning of both the particular and the general. In fact, the ability to relate specific subject matter to higher and more sophisticated levels of causation and significance is a fundamental historical thinking skill. Peter Lee has observed:

> While understanding something in depth is a necessary part of learning history ... it is not enough. Moving from one in-depth topic to another and illuminating each one in the historical spotlight only begins to develop historical understanding if such topics are set in a wider historical framework ... To provide something students can use and think about, we may need to teach a big picture quite quickly, in a matter of two or three weeks, and keep coming back to it. Such a framework focuses on large-scale patterns of change, encompassing students' in-depth studies so they are not simply isolated topics ... This means students need to acquire a usable framework of the past, a big picture organized by substantive concepts they increasingly understand and can reflect upon.[3]

SCALES OF SPACE AND TIME

What is the best way to get started teaching and learning world history? In some curriculums and textbooks, the first major topic is the agricultural revolution in the Fertile Crescent in 12,000 BP (Before Present). In others, the first focus is the founding of river valley civilization in Mesopotamia in 6,000 BP. In modern world history courses, the first topic might be the Renaissance in Europe in the fifteenth and sixteenth centuries. But what if we start, not at a particular spot on the globe, but with the world as a whole? What if we think of the Earth as a "place" whose inhabitants have a shared history? Events and developments may take place inside continents, regions, civilizations, or nation-states, but those "spaces" remain parts of the globe in all its roundness.

Studying the past in this holistic way means asking questions about events and developments that are relatively broad in space and time. In terms of geographical space, study of the history of a rural community, a town, a city, a nation, an empire, a civilization, the world, or even the universe are all valid. It is not that one geographical scale of history is more important than another. Rather, at different scales we can identify and ask different kinds of interesting historical questions. Where one scholar might research 30 years in the history of a Mexican village to understand economic changes there, another might take on migration patterns in Africa south of the Sahara from 1500 to 2000 CE. A third might explore 3,000 years of global climatic change and its effects on human society. Students of world history may study very specific times and events, but they may also try to understand them better by setting them in larger comparative, regional, and global contexts.

We can push this point even farther. The Earth itself is framed by even larger contexts—the solar system, the Milky Way galaxy, and the universe. As we explore how human beings evolved, acquired mental abilities that no other animal species possessed, and came to populate almost all parts of the world, we should remember that when our species emerged, the Earth had already existed for more than four billion years. Complex processes of physical and biological change had long been underway when our first bipedal ancestors appeared on the scene just seven million years ago.

LEARNING TO "THINK THE WORLD"

One of the wonders of our era is that for the first time in history, people everywhere in the world can experience the same event almost simultaneously. A spectacular example of this is the world-wide celebrations that greeted the New Year in 2000. The planet revolved through the time zones, midnight struck again and again, and the festivities broke out in rapid, rolling sequence around the planet. Among the first to celebrate were the people of the Kiribati and Marshall Islands, which lie in the South Pacific just west of the International Date Line. From there, the New Year swept on to Sydney, Beijing, New Delhi, Jerusalem, Lagos, London, Caracas, Seattle, and, at last, Honolulu. Those who had the stamina to watch TV long enough could see the entire relay of parties, prayers, and fireworks displays, for twenty-four straight hours. This spectacle was a compelling reminder of the unity of humankind as inhabitants of a single tiny "marble" suspended in the universe. Also remarkable is that millions of people could consciously witness the world-wide commemoration and reflect upon it in real time.

Electronic marvels invented in the twentieth century enabled men and women to "think the world" in a way that no one could have done in 1000 CE or even in 1900.[4] We live now in what scholars have called a "condition of globality." Careers, family life, community activities, and even mental health all depend to some degree on our understanding of the astonishing complexities that intertwine all human beings. The ability to "think the world"—its economy, science, technology, politics, and culture—must be a primary aim of all education today. This challenges us to rethink humanity's history in a more holistic, interconnected way.

> We live now in what scholars have called a "condition of globality." Careers, family life, community activities, and even mental health all depend to some degree on our understanding of the astonishing complexities that intertwine all human beings.

Millions of young people around the world spend their typical days—when not looking at a computer screen or talking into a cell phone—congregating with family members, fellow students, friends, or coworkers. But those bonds are only our most special. We are also connected, often unconsciously, to numerous other networks of human relationships that affect the course of daily life. Some of these "communities" may be fleeting (passengers sharing an airplane flying at 30,000 feet), and some may be very large (all members of the Roman Catholic Church). Some of them cut across many generations, such as family trees, or the communities formed by particular religions or nations. No individual anywhere in the world is truly isolated from such complex global relationships, not hunters in the Amazon rainforest, nor peasant girls in high Himalayan valleys.

In fact, most people are continuously affected by events and trends initiated in distant parts of the globe. Supermarkets in Wisconsin raise the price of coffee because of weather conditions in Brazil. An office conference call gets cut off, causing minor panic over a deal closure in Beijing. Or, on a very big scale, house prices in the United States drastically drop, triggering a chain of events that ends in a world recession! Our continuous encounters with the wide, wide world are an aspect of the dizzying pace of

Marmite is a yeast paste loved by British children—but not by Americans.

change, the single most conspicuous feature of contemporary life. Whether in the United States, Italy, Burma, or Swaziland, society is perpetually transforming itself because of the growing complexity of world communication, the flow of goods and financial transactions, and the apparently never-ending birth of new ideas, techniques, and products.

Our culture, that is, our language, institutions, laws, moral codes, and regular social routines, buffers us to some extent against the gales of change. Shared culture enables people to have some expectation of how others will think and behave. It helps us predict with at least some accuracy the shape of our affairs from one day to the next. In so far as we have a place in a familiar system of cultural values and organizations, we can usually cope quite well with new things or sudden change. When a social group—a family, religious denomination, business community, or nation—confronts something new or foreign, its members try to fit the strange thing into the existing cultural system with a minimum amount of fuss. Or the group may reject it altogether as useless or distasteful. So far, for example, American children have stoutly resisted Marmite, the yeast paste that British children love to spread on bread. And not everyone in the world likes peanut butter. On the whole, social groups do well at using their cultural yardsticks to sift through the new and strange, accepting one item, rejecting another, so that life does not appear to change all that much from one month to the next.

Yet in today's globally interconnected world, the forces of change, ricocheting around the world, are much more encompassing than we generally realize or wish to believe. Global change is not simply a matter of one event there (war in the Middle East) affecting some condition of life here (a rise in the price of gas). Nor is it just that products or ideas spread quickly from one place to another. The most striking feature of global interaction is that a significant development occurring in one place is likely to set off a complex chain reaction, disrupting and rearranging numerous relationships over an extensive area, maybe even around the world.

When did the world get like this? For how long have peoples of the globe been interconnected? Since the Industrial Revolution? Since World War II? Since the invention of the Internet? A better question might be: How far back in time would we have to go to find a world divided into a collection of entirely separate, self-contained societies, each moving through time along its own track, unresponsive to developments anywhere else? The answer is that we could cast back two hundred, five thousand, twenty thousand years and still not find such a world of completely atomized societies. Indeed, even the early history of humankind hundreds of thousands of years ago is a story of long-distance migrations of hunting and foraging bands across Africa and Eurasia, a process that involved interaction between one group and another wherever such contact took place.

SOME IMPORTANT GEOGRAPHICAL TERMS

To "think world history" in a way that makes room for all peoples requires that we see the spherical surface of the planet as the primary place where history happened. Students need, therefore, to have a basic knowledge of what the World History for Us All model curriculum has called Big Geography, that is, the largest-scale features of the earth's physical and natural environment. These are the patterns of topography, vegetation, climate, and weather that cut across particular nations or cultural groups and that give the world as a whole its distinctive "face." Attention to Big Geography prepares students to explore particular events, time periods, and regions in a way that encourages making connections between whatever subject matter they are learning and the world-scale context. This book uses some geographical terms that may not be familiar to teachers and students.

Afroeurasia

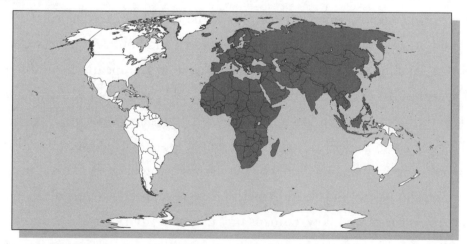

Afroeurasia is the landmass made up of Africa and Eurasia together. Afroeurasia was formed during the last 40 million years by the collision of the tectonic plates that contained Eurasia and those that contained Africa and Arabia. This geographical expression serves as a helpful tool in discussing large-scale historical developments that cut across the traditionally-defined continental divisions of Africa, Asia, and Europe. Even though Africa is separated from both Europe and Asia by the Mediterranean and Red seas (except at the Isthmus of Sinai where modern Egypt meets Israel), these bodies of water have historically been channels of human intercommunication, not barriers to it. Therefore, we may think of both the Mediterranean and the Red Sea as "lakes" inside Afroeurasia.

America, the Americas

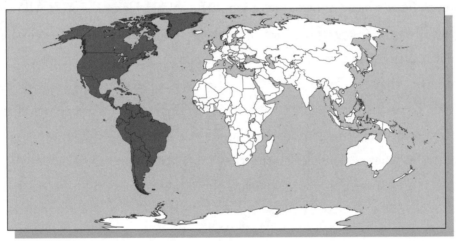

The Americas are made up of the continents of North America and South America, including neighboring islands, notably the islands of the Caribbean Sea. Until the twentieth century, most geography books classified North and South America together as a single continent, labeling them the "New World" ("new" to Europeans beginning in the late fifteenth century CE) in contradistinction to the "Old World," that is, Afroeurasia. In the twentieth century, school children in the United States and most other countries (though not in some Latin American states) were taught to see the "Western Hemisphere" as constituting two continents, joined only by the narrow Isthmus of Panama. On the other hand, humans in North and South America have never been entirely disconnected from one another. As far as we know, humans first migrated from North to South America 12,000 years or longer ago by advancing along either the Isthmus or its coastal waters. Also, it is not hard to perceive the Gulf of Mexico and the Caribbean Sea as two "internal seas" of a single American landmass, much the way we may think of the Mediterranean and Red seas as "inside" Afroeurasia. The Caribbean and the Gulf of Mexico are bounded on three sides by land and on the west by a long string of closely clustered islands.

Australasia

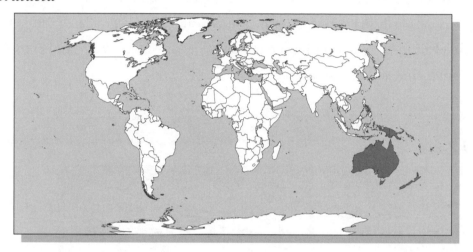

The continent of Australia, plus New Guinea, New Zealand, Tasmania, and other islands that neighbor Australia make up Australasia. During the last Ice Age, when sea levels were lower, Australia, New Guinea, and Tasmania constituted a single landmass known as Sahul. Human settlement of Australasia began as many as 60,000 years ago, though Polynesian mariners did not reach New Zealand until about 1000 CE.

Eurasia

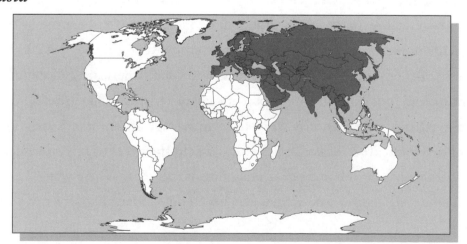

Eurasia is the landmass made up of Asia and Europe. Today, this term is widely used in history and geography education. The idea that Europe and Asia are separate continents goes back many centuries, but scholars who accept the definition of a continent as "a large landmass surrounded, or nearly surrounded, by water" know that the definition applies to neither Europe nor Asia because these two landmasses are conjoined. Moreover, the Ural Mountains, which eighteenth-century European geographers designated as the proper boundary between the European and Asian continents, have never been a serious obstacle to the flow of migrants, armies, trade goods, or ideas. In this book, we define Europe as a subcontinent of Eurasia (or of Afroeurasia), parallel to South Asia or to the Indochinese peninsula.

Great Arid Zone

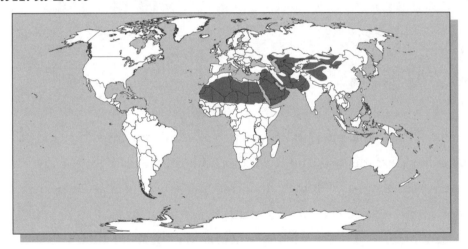

A climatic map of Afroeurasia shows that a good part of the landmass is a belt of dry or semi-dry country that extends all the way from the Atlantic coast of Africa in a generally northeasterly direction to the northern interior of China. This enormous tract comprises a chain of interconnected deserts, mountains, and semi-arid steppes. A steppe may be defined as flat or rolling grassland, equivalent to what Americans call "prairie" and Argentineans call "pampas." The main climatic characteristic of the Great Arid Zone is low annual rainfall, which may range from an average of less than 5 inches in the bleakest of deserts to 20 inches or so in better watered steppes. For several millennia, the Great Arid Zone has been home to pastoral nomadic peoples. Where water has been available from rivers, springs, or wells, it has also been home to farming societies and even large cities.

Indo–Mediterranea

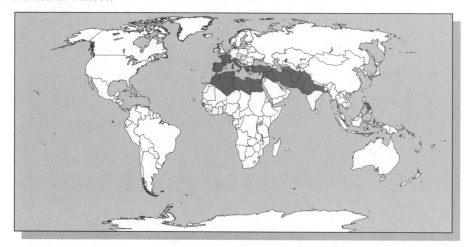

The region of lands and seas extending from the Atlantic coasts of Europe and North Africa to North India is known as Indo-Mediterranea. This expression includes the Mediterranean basin as a whole and extends eastward across Southwest Asia to northern India as far as the Bay of Bengal. In the long term of human history from at least the third millennium BCE to modern times, this region has been characterized by a proliferation of clusters of dense population (notably in river valleys) and by intense commercial and cultural interchange.

Inner Eurasia

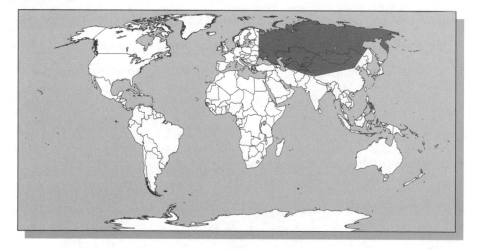

The huge interior landmass of Eurasia, whose dominant features are flat, semi-arid regions of steppe and forest, is known as Inner Eurasia. David Christian defines Inner Eurasia as the territories ruled by the Soviet Union before its collapse, together with

Mongolia and parts of western China. Poland and Hungary on the west and Manchuria (northeastern China) on the east may be thought of as Inner Eurasia's borderlands. The northern margins are boreal forest and Arctic tundra. The southern boundaries are the Himalayas and other mountain chains.

Oceania

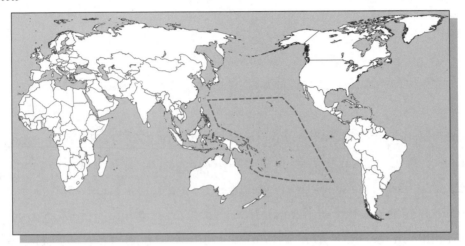

The basin of the Pacific Ocean and its approximately 25,000 islands make up Oceania. Human settlement of this enormous region, sometimes called the Island Pacific, began in western islands near New Guinea about 1600 BCE. Polynesian mariners reached both Hawaii to the northeast and Easter Island to the far southeast around 500 CE. The majority of the islands lie in the tropical belt south of the Equator. The first peoples of Oceania spoke mostly Polynesian languages. Some geographers include both the large island of New Guinea and the continent of Australia as part of Oceania.

Southwest Asia

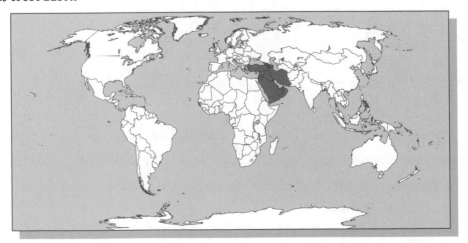

Southwest Asia is the designation of the region, often referred to as the Middle East, which extends from the eastern coast of the Mediterranean Sea to Afghanistan, including Turkey and the Arabian Peninsula, but not including Egypt or any other part of Africa. World History for Us All uses the term "Middle East" only in the context of history since the start of the twentieth century. For earlier periods, "Middle East" has caused students of history considerable confusion because it is used sometimes as a synonym for Southwest Asia, sometimes to encompass Southwest Asia plus Egypt, and sometimes to embrace the entire region from Afghanistan to Morocco.

INTRODUCTION STUDY QUESTIONS

1. What arguments might you make in support of each of the following two ways of learning history?

   • Start with the "big picture" (broad generalizations), and then learn details relevant to it.

   • Start with details (facts, dates, specific information) and then use them to build a big picture.

   What method do you think the scholars quoted in the Introduction are recommending?

2. What reasons would you give for starting to teach and learn world history with each of the following?

   • The beginnings of the universe

   • The appearance of Homo sapiens

   • The first evidence of writing

   • Another period of your own choice

   What is implied in the first three choices about how history is defined? Is the choice of where we think history begins important? Why or why not?

3. Explain what you believe it means to be able to "think the world." How long ago do you believe that people began to be able to "think the world?" What do you believe made "thinking the world" possible?

4. Do you think the geographical concept of Afroeurasia is useful in understanding large-scale events in world history? Why or why not?

5. Why do you think this Introduction emphasizes the importance of studying historical connections and relationships among different peoples and societies? Is a world history approach that investigates one distinct civilization or culture after another an equally valid way of teaching world history? Why or why not?

Big Era One

Humans in the Universe, 13 Billion–200,000 BP

Humans are part of a universe that is older and larger than we can begin to imagine. How was this universe created? How was the earth created? How and when were our ancestors created? What is our place in the universe? Are we important, or are we insignificant?

This Big Era sets the stage for human history. It is about the creation of our environment, of the world we live in, its landscapes, its plants and animals. It is also about the evolutionary steps that led to the creation of our species, Homo sapiens. Understanding this era is vital if we are to grasp how human history fits into the larger history of our earth and the universe as a whole. This is because our ideas about the universe, the earth, and our own existence as a species affect how we think about ourselves and our history. They help us understand our place in the larger universe of which we are a part. So "creation myths," stories that help us understand how everything around us came to be, seem to exist in all human societies.

HUMANS AND THE ENVIRONMENT

In the story of creation in the Bible's Book of Genesis, God made human beings. But he did so only after he had created everything else that was to be part of his universe. The creation took seven days. This is how it began in the biblical account: "And God said, Let there be light: and there was light. And God saw the light, that it was good: and God divided the light from the darkness. And God called the light Day, and the darkness he called Night."[5] After making day and night, God created the seas, dry land, grass,

This infrared image from NASA's Spitzer Space Telescope shows hundreds of thousands of stars crowded into the swirling core of our spiral Milky Way galaxy.

fruit trees, the sun, the moon, fish, birds, cattle, every kind of "creeping thing," and, finally, man and woman. Then he rested.

In thinking about this story, notice that God first made the entire physical and natural environment, everything from the stars to green grass, then fashioned human beings and put them into this setting. In the creation story that modern science tells, the environment was also created before humans, but the time scales are very different. According to modern science, humans evolved on a planet that had already existed for over four-and-a-half billion years. The terrestrial environment shaped the creation of our species. Moreover, the environment of the earth was itself the product of the earlier history of the cosmos as a whole. Consequently, in introducing Big Era One we must begin at the beginning, setting the debut of Homo sapiens within the largest possible scene in both time and space.

The Universe

Modern science suggests that the universe was created about 13.7 billion years BP. What existed before that moment? At present, we have no way of answering that question. Many astronomers would say that the query is meaningless because neither time nor space existed before the creation of the universe. There was nothing. Even so, there must have been at least the possibility of something, because in this "nothingness" a sort of explosion occurred. Within a split second of that explosion, something did exist. The early universe was tiny and fantastically hot, a searing cloud of energy and matter, much hotter than the interior of the sun. For a trillionth of a second the universe expanded faster than the speed of light, until it was bigger than an entire galaxy. Then the rate of expansion slowed, though expansion continues to the present day.

As the universe expanded, it cooled down. After about 300,000 years, it was cool enough that protons and electrons could combine to form atoms of hydrogen and helium. These are the simplest atoms of all. After about one billion years, huge clouds of hydrogen and helium began to collapse in on themselves. As they did so, their centers got hotter and hotter. When they were hot enough, hydrogen atoms began to fuse together violently like vast hydrogen bombs. In this way, the first stars lit up. Hundreds of billions of stars appeared, gathered in hundreds of billions of clusters that we call "galaxies." In the stars, new chemical elements were created, so that as stars lived and died, they generated the energy and

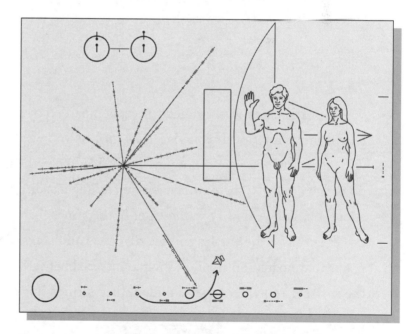

The solar system is depicted at the bottom of this famous NASA plaque mounted on 1972's Pioneer spacecraft, carrying a message to potential extraterrestrials. The arrow at the bottom indicates the spacecraft's trajectory through the planets. Other symbols include naked, friendly humans, neutral hydrogen, and the relative position of the sun to the center of the galaxy.

raw materials needed to make new and more complex types of matter. So it is no accident that complex objects such as planets and human beings appear near stars.

Our Galaxy

Our attention now turns to one tiny part of the universe. Our sun and the planets that circle around it were created about 4.5 billion years BP, so they are about one third of the age of the universe. They were created about two thirds of the way from the center of a galaxy we call the "Milky Way." Look up at the heavens on a clear night, and the Milky Way looks like a pale creamy pathway through the stars.

Our sun is a star, and like all other stars, it was formed from the collapse of a huge cloud of gas and dust particles. More than 99 percent of this material went to make up the sun, but wisps of matter orbited around it at various distances. Over time, the matter in each orbit was drawn together by gravity or by violent collisions into lumps of matter that eventually formed the planets. This is how our earth was formed. At first, it was extremely hot. The heavy metals within it melted and sank to the center of the earth to form its core. Lighter materials rose to the surface, and gases bubbled up to form the earliest atmosphere.

The Earth

The early earth was a violent place, bombarded by asteroids, and bubbling with heat from its interior. If you visited its surface, you would have seen landscapes full of volcanoes. But you would not have been able to breathe because its atmosphere contained no oxygen. Slowly, the number of asteroid impacts diminished, the surface cooled, and, about 4 billion years BP, water vapor in the atmosphere condensed to form the first oceans.

Eventually, the earth's surface hardened and congealed, forming a number of thin plates that floated on the hot, molten material beneath. These plates slowly moved around the surface, and where they collided, they formed huge mountain chains. Where they moved apart, they created huge tears in the earth's surface. You can see one of these tears in Africa's Rift Valley. Some of these huge valleys eventually filled up to form new oceans. This process, known to geologists as "plate tectonics," means that the surface of the earth has changed continuously. As it changed so did the landscapes and weather patterns at the surface of the earth.

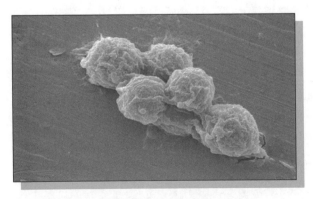

This 2002 scanning electron micrograph (SEM) shows an amoeba in its trophozite phase, a vegetative period spent feeding, moving about, and reproducing.

Early Life Forms

Life evolved in this ever-changing environment. The first living organisms probably evolved deep within the seas. Around volcanic vents at the bottom of oceans, complex chemicals engaged in ever-changing reactions powered by the heat from these volcanoes. Those reactions led to the formation of complex chemicals that eventually created the first living organisms. Did life evolve only on our earth? At present, we do not know for sure. It seems likely, however, that life has evolved many times, wherever planets appeared that are similar to our earth.

The earliest living organisms consisted of single cells, as most living organisms do even today. The earliest organisms probably fed off the chemicals leaking from deep-sea volcanoes. Their fossil remains can be identified today, and the oldest of these remains can be dated to about 3.5 billion years BP. Like all living organisms, those early single-celled creatures were subject to the laws of evolution. Minor changes in organisms were passed on from generation to generation. Those organisms that flourished best in particular environments multiplied most successfully and left the most descendants. In this way, generation by generation, the average features of species gradually changed and diversified, eventually forming entirely new species. And the number and variety of different species increased.

What distinguished the first hominins from other great apes was that they could stand upright. Their brains, however, were about the size of those of modern chimpanzees.

By as early as 3.5 billion years BP, some single-celled organisms began to derive energy directly from sunlight by using the chemical reaction known as photosynthesis. Since then, the sun's energy has been the main "battery" driving life on earth. Photosynthesizing organisms breathed in carbon dioxide and breathed out oxygen. So, as they multiplied, the amount of oxygen in the atmosphere increased. Living organisms were already shaping the earth's atmosphere. Eventually, more complicated cells appeared that

Homo erectus skull

could "breathe" oxygen. These are known as "eukaryotic" cells. From about 600 million years BP, organisms appeared that were made up of many individual eukaryotic cells. These were the first "multi-celled" organisms. Large, multi-celled organisms eventually colonized the land, in the form of plants, fungi, and animals.

Animals

One hundred million years BP, the most flourishing land-based animals were the reptiles we call dinosaurs. About 65 million years BP, however, most of them died off in what was probably a catastrophic meteor impact. Now other types of large animals could flourish in their place. Most successful of all in the last 65 million years has been the large class of animals called mammals. These are warm-blooded, fur-bearing animals that nourish their young in their mothers' wombs and feed their infants with mother's milk. After the dinosaur calamity, mammals began to spread, multiply, and diversify, occupying many of the niches once inhabited by dinosaurs. There appeared grass-eaters, meat-eaters, swimming mammals such as whales, and even flying mammals such as bats.

One family of mammals, the primates, were specialist tree-dwellers. To survive in trees they needed good 3-D vision and a brain large enough to process a lot of visual information. They also needed hands that could grip things with precision. Our own ancestors, the hominins, belonged to a branch of the "great apes," a group of primates that had learned to live at least part of the time on the ground. The first hominins (a term replacing the older word "hominid") appeared about six million years BP, in Africa. What distinguished the first hominins from other great apes was that they could stand upright. Their brains, however, were about the size of those of modern chimpanzees. In Africa, hominins flourished, alongside many other species, and in time a great variety of different hominin species appeared.

Our hominin ancestors used tools known as Acheulean hand axes from about 1.4 million years BP. This specimen was found in France. What useful tasks might an individual have been able to perform with this axe?

HUMANS AND OTHER HUMANS

Early hominins probably lived much like modern chimpanzees or gorillas, that is, in small, family-sized groups that gathered most of their food from plants but also ate insects and small animals. They also occasionally scavenged the meat of larger animals. From about two million years BP, some hominins, from the species known as Homo erectus, migrated out of Africa along the warmer southern fringe of the Eurasian landmass from Europe to China. During the next two million years, new species of hominins appeared in this huge region, some with larger brains. One of those species, known as Neanderthals, flourished in the last 500,000 years.

> **Early hominins probably lived much like modern chimpanzees or gorillas, that is, in small, family-sized groups.**

How did our hominin ancestors live? Like chimpanzees and gorillas, our closest relatives, they were highly social animals that lived in family groups probably ranging from five or six to thirty or forty individuals. We can be pretty sure that they were smart, because chimpanzees are smart. We know they could use and make stone tools because we have found remains of those tools dating from about three million years BP. Modern attempts to make stone tools show how hard the work is, but they also show that using them could make quite a difference to the diets of early hominins. With sharp stone flakes, you could butcher the remains of a large animal very efficiently—as long as the other scavengers, such as hyenas, left you in peace. Using sharpened sticks, maybe hardened in a fire, you could also get at roots of plants. Some early hominins may have used fire. We have strong evidence for the use of fire by hominins living in China in 500,000 BP. Some evidence from Africa suggests that hominins were using fire even earlier than that.

We can also be reasonably sure that early hominin societies were quite complex. Studies of chimpanzee groups today show that they compete for status, making complex alliances with one another to achieve higher standing. Politics of this kind require a lot of "political" intelligence. We also know that chimps care for each other. Mothers have much care for their offspring, and they appear genuinely distraught if their babies come to harm. Hominins almost certainly engaged in behaviors that were equally complex.

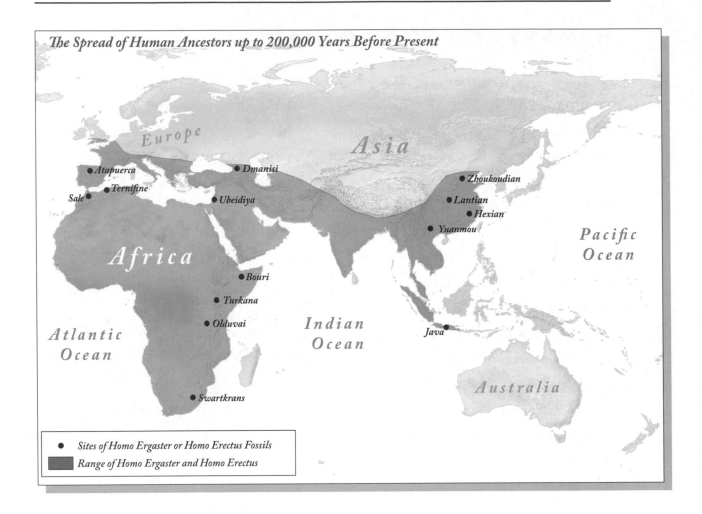

The Spread of Human Ancestors up to 200,000 Years Before Present

• Sites of Homo Ergaster or Homo Erectus Fossils
Range of Homo Ergaster and Homo Erectus

HUMANS AND IDEAS

A varied stone tool kit, elemental social organization, and the control of fire all enabled Homo erectus to become a well-traveled species, one successfully adapted to a large part of the world. Even so, there is still something alien about this creature. Despite its likely successes at social cooperation and competition on a small scale, it did not, as far as we know, evolve complex rules for sharing food, resolving conflicts, or strategizing long-term survival. Homo erectus fossil and tool sites have so far turned up no evidence that they knew anything of symbolic expression, religion, art, or even how to build a simple fireplace. As far as we know, this species produced no wall paintings, no stone carvings, no intentional burial of the dead. In fact, their lifeways changed remarkably little in the two million or more years that they survived, certainly compared to the changes human society has undergone in the past several millennia. The evolutionary processes that produced Homo sapiens, the "wise human" (a name we have given ourselves!), involved not only anatomical changes and greater tool-making skills but also the emergence of social communities that consciously shared a life of symbols, ceremonies, and aesthetic expression.

We may ask, then, why was it that the history of early hominins, like that of chimpanzees, was so different from that of our own species of hominin? Why did these earlier hominins remain confined to Africa and the southern part of Eurasia, never adapting to colder, northerly regions and never reaching Australia or the Americas? Why did they never build villages or cities? Why are chimps still living in roughly the same parts of Africa where their ancestors lived two or three million years BP, and why have their numbers probably remained roughly the same throughout that entire period? Why, by contrast, did Homo sapiens occupy all the great landmasses excepting Antarctica and grow to number more than 6 billion today, living in the vast communities we call cities? In short, what is so different about our own species of hominins? We will take up that question in Chapter 2.

CHAPTER 1 STUDY QUESTIONS

1. "Our ideas about the universe, the earth, and our own existence as a species affect how we think about ourselves and our history." Do you agree or disagree with this statement? Why? What examples can you give of how our ideas about the universe, the earth, and our existence as a species affect us?

2. Historians divide the past into time periods, that is, blocks of time that have certain characteristics different from those of periods that came before and after. How would you divide into time periods the long era from the Big Bang to the first evidence of the existence of Homo sapiens? What events, or what characteristics, would you choose as dividing lines between one period and another? Why?

3. Would you describe the story of change from the Big Bang to the appearance of Homo sapiens as a narrative of increasing complexity, of progress, of recurring cycles, or of something else? Explain your choice. Would you characterize the story of change from the appearance of Homo sapiens to today in the same or a different way? Explain your choice.

4. Which would you describe as the more "successful" life form: single-celled organisms or mammals? Explain your choice. By what characteristics would you measure "success?"

5. What kinds of evidence do scientists use to reconstruct the way early hominins lived? What are possible flaws in this type of evidence that might lead us to wrong conclusions?

1) Yes, we are biased to ourselves being greater, important

3) Increasing Complexity because we see more and more difficult things happening, one leading to the next

Networks:
- Small connections become large
- Connection of World, Inetwork

Big Era Two

Human Beings Almost Everywhere, 200,000–10,000 BP

This is the first era in which our own species, Homo sapiens, is known to have existed. Therefore, it is the first era of human history. Scholars argue vigorously about when Homo sapiens first appeared. An increasing number of archaeologists and paleontologists think that this happened about 200,000 BP, in eastern Africa. One reason supporting this approximate date is that today the genetic differences between humans are very small, far too small for those differences to have accumulated over a period much longer than 200,000 years. Also, fossilized remains of humans from almost 200,000 BP suggest that they were almost identical to the anatomies of people living today. There are also hints that those folk were beginning to behave very differently from earlier hominins.

Big Era Two extends to about 10,000 BP when, in some parts of the world, humans began for the first time to take up farming. Scholars conventionally mark that date as the approximate transition from the Paleolithic (Old Stone Age) to the Neolithic (New Stone Age). That is when humans in some places started using an array of more sophisticated stone tools, many of which assisted in early agricultural production. So we can think of Big Era Two as the era of human history that preceded farming and agriculture.

This era before farming was by far the longest in human history—embracing about 95 percent of the time that our species has existed on earth—but it is also the era we know least about. So in discussing it we will have to explore the different types of evidence used to try to understand it.

Most historical scholarship is based on written evidence. Writing did not exist during Big Era Two, however, so we cannot tell a traditional historical story about this period. For example, we do not know the names of a single society or individual from that era.

Nevertheless, scholars have done a great deal of research in archaeology. Therefore, we can say a surprising amount about how humans lived and how they related to the natural environment. We can even make some reasonable guesses about how they thought about the external world around them. Archaeologists are extremely skillful at examining material objects that have survived from this era in order to help us understand how people lived. For example, scholars can learn much by examining the bones of both humans and the animals humans hunted. Archaeologists also analyze the remains of human tools or foods. They can often date these remains quite accurately. They can therefore study how technologies changed over time and how humans slowly spread into new areas. They also use what they know about climatic change to make inferences about changes in human life. Finally, study of modern communities that use technologies similar to those known in Big Era Two can give us some helpful hints about the way people lived, the organization of their communities, and the sort of perceptions they may have had about their world.

In recent years, scientists have discovered a major new source for reconstructing early human history, especially the dating and patterns of migratory movements. This tool is the analysis of DNA (deoxyribonucleic acid), the material inside the nucleus of a cell that carries genetic information for reproduction of cells. Scientists can determine the DNA profile of any individual by drawing a blood sample or taking a swab of cells from inside a person's mouth. As DNA flows from one generation of humans to the next, small alterations, or mutations occur. This happens at a regular rate, which means that over time the genetic differences between individuals sharing a common ancestor statistically increase. The longer two human populations have no contact with one another, the greater the genetic differences between them will be. Using complicated biochemical procedures, scientists can measure the rate of change in genetic material and therefore estimate how long ago in thousands or even tens of thousands of years two human groups separated from each other. From this data, scholars may propose hypotheses about early migratory directions and dating.

> **Language may in fact be the defining characteristic of our species.**

To understand how people might have been thinking before 10,000 BP, we have to resort mostly to indirect forms of evidence. If people buried their dead, it is tempting to think that they had an idea of an afterlife and were, in some sense, religious. Art, however, provides probably the most powerful evidence of how humans perceived their world. Most archaeologists believe that the existence of art is one of the first signs that humans had a wider, more complex ability to communicate. So, when we find early evidence of art, we are probably in the presence of people who were capable of using language.

Language may in fact be the defining characteristic of our species. Apart from the evidence of bones, how can we tell that early Homo sapiens really were fully human? In fact, what is it that distinguishes humans from animals? Historians, philosophers, and archaeologists have debated this basic question for a long time, and they have not reached a universally accepted answer. One trait that appears on most lists of what makes us human is the ability to communicate with one another through language.

Bone fish hooks found in western Europe and dated between 25,000 and 15,000 BP

Many animals can use gestures to communicate with each other, but only humans can communicate information with precision and detail. Only humans can talk about things that are not present (a new pathway through a forest), things that probably do not exist (dragons, leprechauns, or sky gods), things that are abstract (one o'clock in the afternoon or the beauty of a ripe pear). Because of this ability, humans can communicate to one another the results of what they learn in their lifetime. And that means that within each community, knowledge could accumulate as each individual and each generation contributed to the common store of knowledge. This transformed the relationship of humans to their environment and to each other.

HUMANS AND THE ENVIRONMENT

All animals learn how to get food and other resources from their environment. When an animal dies, however, almost all the knowledge it has accumulated in its lifetime dies with it. The ability of humans to communicate very precisely with each other changed that rule. The things that individuals learned during their lifetime could now be passed on to others. This meant that new knowledge could be stored up and handed on to the next generation. So humans, unlike all other animals, slowly accumulated more and more new ways of dealing with their environment and preserving what they knew. They could add to their knowledge from one century to another. This process, which we call "collective learning," explains many of the distinctive features of the history of our species.

One of the earliest signs of the presence of modern humans is an acceleration in the pace of technological change. The stone tools of the earlier hominins show little change in the course of a million years or more. But once humans appear, so do new types of tools. These implements are more varied, more delicately made, and more precisely designed for specific tasks. By modern standards, the pace of technological change was still slow. Nevertheless, Big Era Two witnessed changes that have transformed human history at an accelerating speed ever since.

Adaptation and Migration

As technologies changed, people learned to live in more varied environments. By 100,000 BP, Homo sapiens had already learned to live in places, such as deserts and dense forests, that no earlier hominins had occupied. Later, modern humans began to explore environments outside their African homeland. From about 100,000 BP, we have evidence of modern humans inhabiting Southwest Asia (the Middle East), and then over the following 80,000 to 90,000 years migrating to most other regions of Afroeurasia and to Australia and the Americas.

> One of the earliest signs of the presence of modern humans is an acceleration in the pace of technological change.

In recent years evidence has been accumulating to suggest that the earliest bands of foragers, that is, communities that made a living by hunting and gathering food, made their way eastward across Eurasia. Evidence from DNA suggests that humans departed from Africa by an easterly route starting in perhaps 70,000 BP, moving around the rim of the Arabian Sea to India, and eventually from there around the Bay of Bengal to Southeast Asia and China. We do not know if they had rafts or canoes, but they may well have had some kind of craft because open water separated northeastern Africa from the Arabian Peninsula even during the last Ice Age, or Pleistocene, when much water was locked up in glaciers and sea levels were 200 feet lower than they are today. Forager bands making their way across Eurasia could have thrived, multiplied, and made rapid progress (on a scale of thousands of years) because they did not have to face radically varying ecological conditions if they kept to tropical coastlands. They would have had an abundant and nutritious diet of edible plants, fish, and seafood. Traces of their campsites and boats may now lie deep under water because sea levels rose after the Ice Age began to recede in about 18,000 BP.

Perhaps in 60,000 BP or even earlier, some humans crossed a short expanse of sea to settle on the continent of Sahul, a landmass that at that time joined together Australia and Papua New Guinea. From perhaps 40,000 BP, humans began to occupy the cold lands of Russia and Ukraine. From there, they migrated into the even icier environments of Siberia. In such cold climates, they needed highly specialized technologies. They built pit houses and learned to sew warm clothing using bone needles. They also learned to be very efficient hunters. Because plant foods were scarce, they had to learn how to hunt huge animals such as mammoths.

At least by 15,000 BP and very likely thousands of years earlier, some humans crossed the Bering Strait from eastern Siberia into the Americas. Once in the Western Hemisphere, they spread from northern Canada to the southern end of South America within one or two thousand years. Scholars have recently argued that humans accomplished this feat in as short a time as they did because the first peoples who inhabited the western coast lands of the Americas thrived on a rich marine diet. As their numbers grew, they migrated steadily southward in small boats. Archeological evidence from a site in Virginia suggests that humans also crossed North America overland, arriving at the Atlantic seaboard as long ago as 15,000 BP.

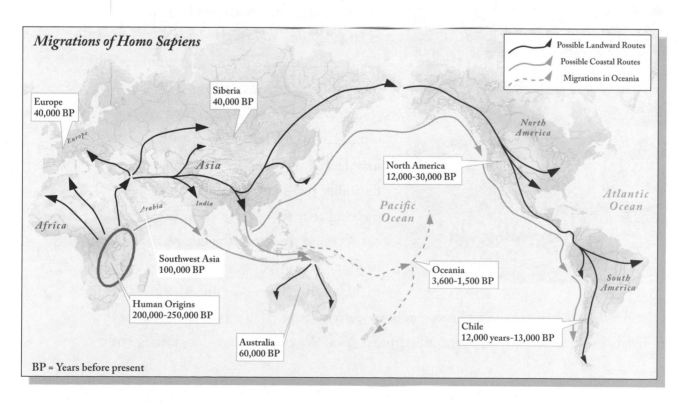

Migrations of Homo Sapiens

Possible Landward Routes
Possible Coastal Routes
Migrations in Oceania

Europe
40,000 BP

Siberia
40,000 BP

North
America

Asia

North America
12,000–30,000 BP

Pacific
Ocean

Atlantic
Ocean

Arabia   India

Africa

Southwest Asia
100,000 BP

Oceania
3,600–1,500 BP

South
America

Human Origins
200,000–250,000 BP

Chile
12,000 years–13,000 BP

Australia
60,000 BP

BP = Years before present

HUMANS POPULATE THE MAJOR LANDMASSES OF THE WORLD

Humans' Environmental Impact

In Australia, Siberia, and the Americas, humans found many new species of animals and plants. In these regions, animals had never encountered humans before, and many species underestimated how dangerous this strange new two-legged creature was. Consequently, the first human colonists found hunting easy. This may explain why many large animal species—the mammoths of Siberia, the giant wombats and emus of Australia, the horses and saber-toothed tigers of the Americas—soon became extinct. Humans also learned to use fire to burn vegetation and encourage new plant growth, thereby attracting the plant-eating animals that they wanted to hunt. By regularly setting fire to the land and by over-hunting, humans began to have a significant impact on the natural environment wherever they settled.

> Perhaps the most striking illustration of how dangerous modern humans could be was the disappearance of all other hominin species. Neanderthals, and perhaps some types of Homo erectus, survived throughout much of Big Era Two.

Perhaps the most striking illustration of how dangerous modern humans could be was the disappearance of all other hominin species. Neanderthals, and perhaps some types of Homo erectus, survived throughout much of Big Era Two. These species may even have met groups of Homo sapiens. Neanderthals had brains at least as large as ours, and they were effective hunters. But it seems they could not communicate with each other nearly as well as modern humans could. We have no evidence that they had the gift of language. They appear, therefore, to have lacked the remarkable adaptability and flexibility that modern humans had owing to their capacity for collective learning.

As far as we know, the last Neanderthals lived in the south of France, perhaps in 25,000 to 30,000 BP. There are hints that they tried, and failed, to imitate the technologies of modern humans. Other hominins may have lived almost as recently in parts of Southeast Asia. We cannot know for certain, but it seems likely that, as modern humans occupied more and more territory, close genetic relatives living in those regions were slowly driven to extinction.

By 10,000 BP, humans could be found in all the world's big landmasses—Afroeurasia, Australia, and the Americas. As the area that humans occupied expanded, their numbers probably increased as well. Yet the size of each community likely remained small. In other words, population increased by "extensification," that is, by increasing the number of communities and the area of settlement across the world without increasing the size of each community. By contrast, "intensification," which means increasing the size of each community and the numbers living within a given area, would become more important in Big Era Three after farming came into use. But even the slow population growth of Big Era Two may have raised the total number of humans from a few hundred thousand to a few millions. If so, the population world-wide at the end of the era was 1/1000th its size today.

HUMANS AND OTHER HUMANS

How did people live in Big Era Two? Archaeologists can tell us a lot about their dwellings and the tools they used, but it is harder to understand their social and cultural lives. We are sure that virtually all people were gatherers, hunters, or fishers in that era, even though the techniques people employed continued to vary and multiply as groups settled more widely across the globe.

Social Life in the Paleolithic Era

We may be able to gain insight into the social and economic lives of Big Era Two peoples by investigating the lifeways of those few modern societies that continue to survive by hunting and gathering. Scholars have to use this kind of evidence cautiously because we certainly cannot assume that modern foragers live generally the same way that their predecessors did 10,000 to 200,000 years BP! We can, however, use modern evidence to advance some hypotheses. Today's forager communities make up a minuscule percentage of the world's population, but they persist in a few places on all the continents. Except in extremely cold environments, they rely mainly on gathered plants for subsistence. Meat is valued, and most communities have hunters who occasionally bring it

Sites uncovered in Russia and the Ukraine have revealed hamlets where people dug "pit houses," then ringed them with mammoth bones and covered the structure with hides to keep out the cold. This picture is a modern reconstruction of a type of pit house that existed perhaps 12,000 to 18,000 BP. In designing an accurate reconstruction of a pit house that fell apart thousands of years ago, what sort of historical evidence might scholars have used, and how?

in. But meat is not the main component of most forager diets because hunting is usually less reliable than gathering.

In cold environments such as the Arctic where plant foods are scarce, people rely on the meat from seals, whales, and caribou. Their hunting techniques have to be extremely sophisticated. All foragers have to have deep knowledge about the plants and animals they use. Most modern forager communities are mobile, traveling through the land as the seasons change and staying in a single camp for only a few weeks before moving on. The largest communities are really large families, that is, groups of ten to forty or fifty people who travel together and periodically encounter other groups. When they meet, individuals often move from one group to another because of marriages, quarrels, or even boredom.

The main divisions within these forager communities are of age and gender. Men and women often have different economic and social roles, as do the old and the young, but there are few differences in wealth and power because no one stores up wealth. It does not make sense to do that if you can find the things you need all around you. And besides, if you are traveling much of the time, why try to carry many possessions with you? By combining the knowledge we have of modern foragers with the evidence of archaeology (stone tools and weapons, human and animal bones, and the remains of camp sites), we can construct a broad picture of how people lived during Big Era Two.

The Beginnings of Permanent Settlement

Towards the end of the era, we start finding signs that some communities were spending more time at particular sites and becoming more settled. This may have happened earliest in coastal areas where marine food resources were particularly abundant. As communities stayed longer in a single place, they devised new ways to increase their food supply. For example, they might care for stands of favored food plants by clearing weeds or scaring away birds. Or, they might build weirs (enclosures set in a waterway) to stock fish or eels. These technological innovations had features that were at least faintly characteristic of farming, the technology that appeared in Big Era Three.

> **The [hunter gatherers] are really large families, that is, groups of ten to forty or fifty people who travel together and periodically encounter other groups.**

Was foraging life 10,000 years or longer ago "nasty, brutish, and short," as the English philosopher Thomas Hobbes thought, or was it reasonably comfortable? On one hand, it is probable that many people died young from illnesses, childbirth crises, or hunting expeditions gone bad. On the other hand, studies of modern hunter-gatherers suggest that in Big Era Two humans had a varied and nutritionally-adequate diet, as well as much more leisure time in a day than farmers have traditionally had. So, for a person born into a forager community, that mode of living was probably both satisfying and fulfilling.

HUMANS AND IDEAS

Modern forager communities often think of the world as a place full of many different types of intelligent beings besides humans. Peoples who lived in Big Era Two may have thought the same thing. Some cave and rock paintings, as well as sculptured objects of stone, bone, or ivory, survive from the era. Many of the paintings depict hunting, but some artistic expressions also hint at various kinds of magical, supernatural beliefs. These pictures are hard to interpret, but they seem to describe a world full of spirits—spirits that animate stones, mountains, lakes, trees, and animals. If this is the case, then it is probable that humans in Big Era Two thought of themselves as just one part of the natural world. They had none of the sense of separateness from nature that characterizes religions and cosmologies in later eras of history.

> Cave paintings and carved objects were just one of the ways that women and men expressed themselves symbolically through art.

The Earliest Art

Cave paintings and carved objects were just one of the ways that women and men expressed themselves symbolically through art. An early hint of the existence of art among humans is the physical evidence of powdered pigments. People appear to have ground up pigments, such as ochre, and used them to paint themselves or their surroundings. In fact, evidence of ground pigment use in southern Africa dates to well over 100,000 BP. Therefore, we may also have an early date for the use of language.

Archaeologists have unearthed tantalizing evidence of advanced technical skill and symbolic thinking at sites in Africa. In 2007, scientists working in eastern Morocco announced the discovery of perforated marine shell beads that they believe are 82,000 years old. These trinkets are colored with red ochre, and some of them show wear patterns suggesting that people suspended them from a cord. A site called Twilight Cave

This scene was painted in natural pigments on the wall of a cave in Lascaux, France. The painting is dated between 12,000 and 17,000 BP.

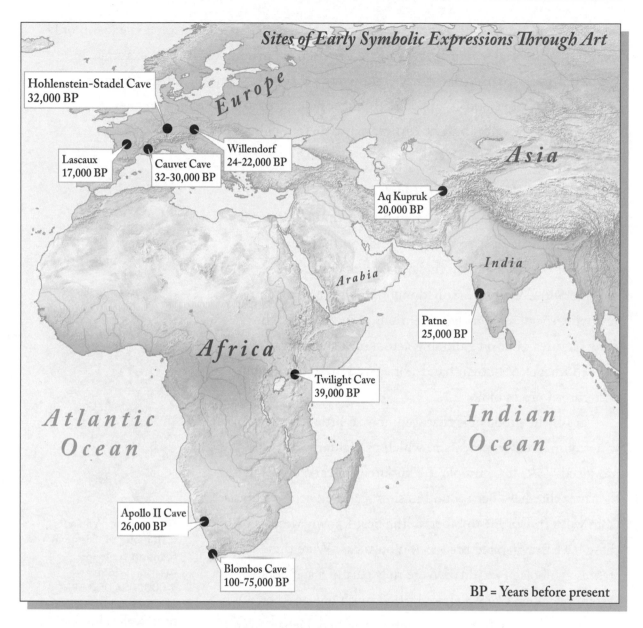

Sites of Early Symbolic Expressions Through Art

Hohlenstein-Stadel Cave
32,000 BP

Europe

Asia

Lascaux
17,000 BP

Cauvet Cave
32-30,000 BP

Willendorf
24-22,000 BP

Aq Kupruk
20,000 BP

India

Arabia

Patne
25,000 BP

Africa

Twilight Cave
39,000 BP

*Atlantic
Ocean*

*Indian
Ocean*

Apollo II Cave
26,000 BP

Blombos Cave
100-75,000 BP

BP = Years before present

in Kenya has revealed ostrich eggshell beads dated to about 40,000 BP. Men and women appear to have been making and wearing beads from South Africa to the shores of the Mediterranean thousands of years before our species ventured to other parts of the world.

In any case, between about 50,000 to 10,000 BP, the period scholars call the Upper Paleolithic, artistic expression burst forth in many parts of the world. Humans began to produce not only paintings and carvings but also necklaces, bracelets, pendants, beads, and ornamental headgear. Through this art women and men represented their world symbolically.

Wherever people lived, they took advantage of the local materials and opportunities they had. Wall painting, for example, is concentrated heavily in northern Spain and southwestern France where deep limestone caves provided "gallery space" protected from rain and wind. In Eastern Europe, by contrast, cave shelters are rare, so people commonly carved small, portable figurines. Humans even started making music. For example, in western Eurasia archaeologists have found more than thirty flute-like instruments made of long hollow bone and equipped with finger holes. Most of these instruments are broken and unplayable, but the earliest may date to roughly 37,000 BP.

Interpreting Ancient Art Objects

Explaining the meaning of painting, sculpture, or music is always risky because so much depends on the cultural context of the work and on the ideas we ourselves bring to the interpretation. We can hardly do more than speculate on the aesthetic, social, or spiritual intentions of individuals who drew pictures of bison galloping across rock shelter walls, painted images of human hands, or carved mysterious spiral patterns on pieces of bone.

Part of the problem is that we know so little about the wider human environments in which particular works were produced. Take for example the hundreds of carved "Venus" figurines that have been found in sites scattered across Eurasia from western Europe to Siberia. The best-known samples of these have exaggerated breasts and buttocks. Were these female statues symbols of fertility? Were they part of a symbolic system by which women shared rituals with one another? Did their meaning vary from one region to another? Debate over the meaning of art in the Upper Paleolithic will continue for a long time.

The Venus of Willendorf, a statuette of limestone found at a site in Austria. It dates to 24,000–26,000 BP. What meaning might people who possessed or looked at this statue have attributed to it?

We have no material artifacts at all to help us understand the most important sign systems of all, spoken languages. Writing presumably lay far in the future. Or did it? We do have quite a bit of evidence from the Upper Paleolithic of abstract markings, such as dots, paired lines, and zigzags. These signs seem to suggest systematic storing or transmitting of information, perhaps a record of hunting successes or the phases of the moon. If such symbols were early forms of writing, we still cannot connect the marks to sounds that came out of people's mouths. We also know almost nothing about the development and spread of particular spoken languages in Big Era Two. We may assume, though, that this was taking place as global colonization proceeded.

CHAPTER 2 STUDY QUESTIONS

1. What kinds of evidence support the idea that anatomically-modern Homo sapiens acquired language early in its history?

2. From what types of evidence have we been able to build knowledge about early Homo sapiens' behavior, thinking, way of life, and migrations? Which types of evidence would you consider the most reliable? Explain your choice.

3. Think about some of the reasons for migrations in the contemporary world. Which of them, if any, would have influenced the migrations of Homo sapiens in Big Era Two?

4. What evidence can you give for the claim that human societies became more culturally diverse during Big Era Two? What factors might have contributed to greater cultural diversity among human communities?

5. How do you think environmental conditions and ways of life might have influenced symbolic expression and art-making during the period from about 100,000 to 10,000 BP?

Big Era Three

Farming and the Emergence of Complex Societies, 10,000–1000 BCE

About 10,000 BCE (12,000 BP) some human communities began to move in a new direction. For the first time, they began to produce food in a systematic way rather than hunt or collect all their food in the wild. The emergence of farming and the far-reaching social and cultural changes that came with it sets Big Era Three apart from the first two.

From one perspective, the advent of farming was a slow, fragmented process. It happened independently in several different parts of the world at different times. It occurred as a result of people making thousands of minute decisions about food production without anyone being conscious that humans were "inventing agriculture." And even though some people started farming, others continued for thousands of years to live entirely on wild resources or to combine crop growing with hunting and gathering.

From another perspective we might argue that agriculture took the world by storm. The Paleolithic era of hominin and human tool-making went on for about two million years. Farming settlements, however, appeared on all the major landmasses except Australia within a mere 8,000 years. Foraging societies may have retreated gradually, but today, just 12,000 years after the first signs of agriculture, they have all but disappeared.

We may define farming as a set of interrelated activities that increase the production of those resources that humans can use, such as cattle, grain, or flax, and reduce the production of things humans cannot use, such as weeds or pests. In order to increase the production of resources they can use, farmers systematically manipulate their environment, removing those species they do not want and creating conditions that allow the species they favor to flourish. Thus, we plow and water the land so that our crops can thrive, and we provide food and protection to the animals we need. This is why the emergence of societies based on agriculture, what we call agrarian societies, involved a complex interplay of plants, animals, topography, climate, and weather with human tools, techniques, social habits, and cultural understandings.

The fundamental technological element of this interplay was domestication, the ability to alter the genetic makeup of plants and animals to make them more useful to humans. Scholars have traditionally labeled the early millennia of agriculture the Neolithic era (meaning "new stone age"), because humans developed a more varied and sophisticated kit of stone tools in connection with the emergence of farming.

> **Systematic food production contributed hugely to the amazing biological success of Homo sapiens.**

Systematic food production contributed hugely to the amazing biological success of Homo sapiens. In our discussion of Big Era Two, we introduced the concept of extensification, the idea that in Paleolithic times humans multiplied and flourished by spreading thinly across the major landmasses of the world (excepting Antarctica) and by adapting to a wide range of environments, from equatorial forests to Arctic tundra. In Big Era Three, however, a process of "intensification" got under way. This meant that by producing resources from domesticated plants and animals, humans could settle and thrive on a given land area in much greater numbers and density than ever before.

The consequences of intensification were astonishing. In the 9,000 years of Big Era Three, world population rose from about 6 million to about 120 million, a change involving a much faster rate of increase than in the previous eras. Such growth, in turn, required unprecedented experiments in human organization and ways of thinking.

HUMANS AND THE ENVIRONMENT

Scholars generally agree that foragers of the Paleolithic enjoyed, at least much of the time, sufficient food supplies, adequate shelter, and shorter daily working hours than most adults do today. Humans did not, therefore, consciously take up crop growing and animal raising because they thought they would have a more secure and satisfying life. In other words, humans seem to have been "pushed" into agriculture rather than "pulled" into it.

When some communities in certain places made the transition to farming, they did it incrementally over centuries or even millennia, and they had no clear vision that they were dropping one whole way of life for another. If we can speak of an "agricultural revolution," we would also have to say that humans backed slowly into it even if, on the scale of 200,000 years, the change was rapid.

The Great Thaw

The coming of agrarian societies was almost certainly connected to the waning of the Pleistocene, or Ice Age, the period beginning at about 15,000 BP when glaciers shrank and both sea levels and global temperatures rose. In several parts of the Northern Hemisphere rainfall increased significantly. This period of 5,000 to 7,000 years was the prelude to the Holocene, the climatic epoch that spans most of the last 10,000 years. Rising seas drowned low-lying coastal shelves as well as land bridges that had previously connected regions separated by water today. Land bridges now under water included spans between Siberia and Alaska, Australia and Papua New Guinea, and Britain and continental Europe.

One consequence of this "great thaw" was the dividing of the world into three distinct zones, whose human populations, as well as other land-bound animals and plants, had very limited contact with one another. These zones were 1) Afroeurasia and adjacent islands, that is Africa, Asia, and Europe combined; 2) the Americas; and 3) Australia. From about 4000 BCE, the Pacific Ocean basin and its island populations began to emerge as a fourth distinct zone. Though humans rarely had contact between one zone and another (until 1500 CE or later), within each of the zones they interacted more or less intensively, depending on patterns of geography, climate, and changing historical circumstances.

> **The natural bounty was so great in some localities that human bands began to settle in one place all or part of the year to forage and hunt.**

A second consequence of the great thaw was that across much of the Northern Hemisphere, warmer, rainier, ice-free conditions permitted forests, meadowlands, and small animal populations to flourish. The natural bounty was so great in some localities that human bands began to settle in one place all or part of the year to forage and hunt. That is, they became sedentary, settled in hamlets or villages rather than moving from camp to camp. For example, in the relatively well-watered part of Southwest Asia we call the Fertile Crescent, groups began sometime between 10,000 and 13,000 BP to found tiny settlements in order to collect plentiful stands of wild grain and other edible plants and animals.

The Dawn of Domestication

In time, these groups took up the habit of protecting their wild grain fields against weeds, drought, and birds. Eventually they started broadcasting edible plant seeds onto new ground to increase the yield. Finally, they began selecting and planting seeds from individual plants that seemed most desirable for their size, taste, and nutrition. In other words, humans learned how to control and manipulate the reproduction of plants that were bigger, tastier, more nutritious, and easier to grow, harvest, store, and cook than were wild food plants. Systematic domestication was under way!

In the Fertile Crescent, key domesticates included the ancestors of wheat, barley, rye, and several other edible plants. Selecting and breeding particular animal species—sheep, goats, cattle, pigs—that were good to eat and easy to manage occurred in a similar way. In effect, humans started grooming the natural environment to reduce the organisms they did not want (weeds, predatory wolves) and to increase the number of organisms they did want (grains, legumes, wool-bearing sheep, hunting dogs).

Co-Dependency

Eventually, plant-growing and animal-raising communities became "co-dependent" with their domesticates. That is, humans came to rely on these genetically altered species to survive. In turn, domesticated plants and animals were so changed that they would thrive only if humans took care of them. For example, the maize, or corn, that we see in fields today can no longer reproduce without human help.

The great advantage of co-dependency was that a community could rely fairly predictably on a given area of land to produce sufficient, even surplus, yields of hardy, tasty food. Populations of both humans and their domesticates tended to grow accordingly. On the darker side, co-dependency was a kind of trap: a farming community, which had to huddle together in a crowded village and labor long hours in the fields, could not go back to a foraging way of life even if it wanted to. And, as we will see, a lot of new problems appeared as humans began to live together in denser communities, from new types of diseases to the buildup of village waste and rubbish.

Environmental Intervention

The Fertile Crescent was an early incubator of agriculture, but it was by no means the only one. Between 12,000 and 3000 BCE, similar processes involving a great variety of domesticates occurred in several different parts of the world. The intensification in population densities and economic productivity that farming permitted also spurred humans to intervene in the natural and physical environment as never before. As farmers cleared more land, planted more crops, and pastured more animals, they enhanced their species' biological success. That is, there occurred a positive feedback cycle of ever-increasing population and productivity that looked something like this:

Beginning about 6000 BCE, intensification in particular parts of the world moved to a level that required radical innovations in the way humans lived and worked.

Crowded Cities

First in the Tigris-Euphrates and Nile River valleys, then the Indus valley, and later in China's Huang River (Huang He) valley and a few other regions, societies emerged that were far larger and denser than the farming communities of the Neolithic period. We refer to these big concentrations of people as complex societies, or, more traditionally, as civilizations.

Their most conspicuous characteristic was cities. Early cities were centers of power, manufacturing, and creativity. Building and preserving them, however, required drastic alterations of the local environment to produce sufficient food, building materials, and sources of energy. The price of this intervention was high. Dense urban societies were extremely vulnerable to changes in weather, climate, disease conditions, wood supplies, and trade links to distant regions. After the appearance of complex societies, humans stepped up their efforts to manipulate and control their physical and natural environment. This had great benefits but also produced a negative feedback cycle.

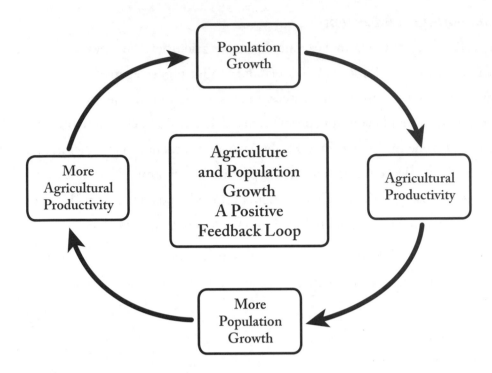

- Deforestation and consequent erosion threatened periodic food shortages and social conflict.

- Habitation in densely packed villages and cities brought humans in closer contact with disease-carrying animals, resulting in greater vulnerability to epidemic infections.

- In the cases of some complex societies, ecological problems stimulated social and economic innovations to improve conditions or stave off disaster. In some other cases, however, these problems led eventually to economic, demographic, or political collapse.

As farmers cleared more land, planted more crops, and pastured more animals, they enhanced their species' biological success.

HUMANS AND OTHER HUMANS

The intensification of population and production that came with Big Era Three obliged humans to experiment with new forms of social organization. The customs and rules that governed social relationships in a foraging band of twenty-five or thirty people were no longer adequate.

The permanent farming settlements that multiplied in Afroeurasia in the early millennia of the era numbered as few as several dozen people to as many as 10,000. These communities had to work together in more complicated ways and on a larger scale than was the case in foraging bands. Even so, social relations may not have changed greatly from foraging days. Men and women probably continued to treat each other fairly equally. No one had a full-time job other than farming. Some individuals no doubt became leaders because they were strong or intelligent. No individual or group, however, had formal power to lord over the rest.

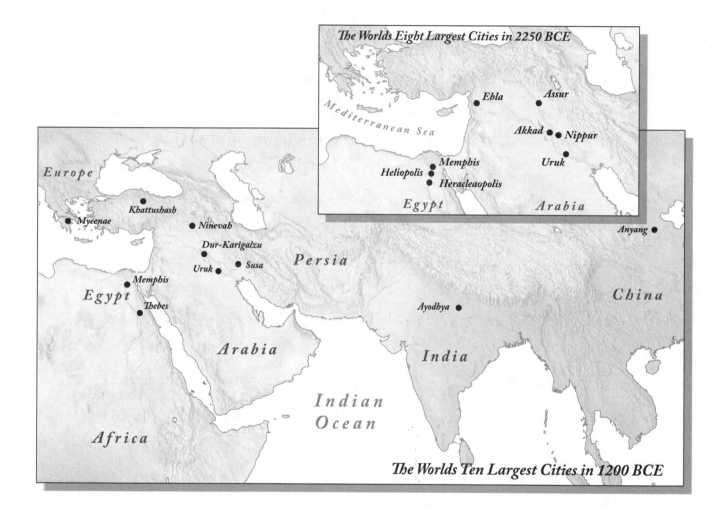

Early Complex Societies

Only after about 4000 BCE did truly staggering changes occur in social customs and institutions. The complex societies that arose in the Tigris-Euphrates, Nile, and Indus valleys, and somewhat later in other regions, were cauldrons of intensification. That is, people lived and worked together in much larger, denser communities than had ever existed. These societies shared a number of fundamental characteristics, which we generally associate with civilizations:

- Cities arose, the early ones varying somewhat in their forms and functions. By 2250 BCE, there were about eight cities in the world that had 30,000 or more inhabitants. By 1200 BCE, there were about sixteen cities that big.

- Some people took up full-time specialized occupations and professions (artisans, merchants, soldiers, priests, and so on) rather than spending most of their time collecting, producing, or processing food.

- A hierarchy of social classes appeared in which some men and women—the elite class—had more wealth, power, and privilege than did others. Also, men became dominant over women in political and social life, leading to patriarchy.

- The state, that is, a centralized system of government and command, was invented. This meant that a minority group—kings, queens, high officials, priests, generals—exercised control over the labor and social behavior of everyone else.

- Complex exchanges of food and other products took place within the complex society, and lines of trade connected the society to neighbors near and far.

- Technological innovations multiplied, and each new useful invention tended to suggest several others.

- Monumental building took place—city walls, temples, palaces, public plazas, and tombs of rulers.

- A system of writing, or at least a complex method of record-keeping, came into use.

- Spiritual belief systems, public laws, and artistic expressions all became richer and more complex.

- Creative individuals collaborated with the ruling class to lay the foundations of astronomy, mathematics, and chemistry, as well as civil engineering and architecture.

A society did not have to exhibit every one of these characteristics to qualify as a civilization. The checklist is less important than the fact that all these social, cultural, economic, and political elements interacted dynamically with one another. The synergism among them made the society complex, that is, made it recognizable as a civilization.

A copper bull from the Sumerian site of Al-Ubaid, in modern-day southern Iraq. It is dated to about 2600 BCE. Why do you think people made objects of copper earlier than any other metal?

Animal-Herding Societies

From about the fourth millennium BCE, Afroeurasia saw the development of a new type of society and economy in parts of the Great Arid Zone. This is the belt of dry and semi-arid land that extends across Afroeurasia from the Sahara Desert in the west to Manchuria in northern China. Here, communities began to organize themselves around a specialized way of life based on herding domesticated animals, whether sheep, cattle, horses, or camels. Known as pastoral nomadism, this economic system permitted humans to adapt in larger numbers than ever before to climates where intensive farming was not possible. Pastoral nomads lived mainly on the products of their livestock—meat, milk, blood, hides, hair, wool, and bone. They often grazed and migrated over extensive areas, and they planted crops either not at all or as a minor, supplemental activity.

By the third millennium BCE, animal-breeding societies were appearing in a number of regions, notably along the margins of the Great Arid Zone. These communities found they could adapt to dry conditions because sheep, cattle, and a few other domesticates could thrive on wild grasses and shrubs. These animals converted vegetable matter that humans could not digest into meat, milk, and blood, which they could. That is, humans became experts at transforming the natural flora of arid lands into an animal diet high in protein and fat.

Pastoral communities usually followed regular migratory routes from pasture to pasture as the seasons changed. When families were on the move, they lived in hide tents or other movable dwellings, and their belongings had to be limited to what they could carry along. This does not mean that they wished to cut themselves off from farming societies or cities. Rather, pastoralists eagerly purchased farm produce or manufactures in exchange for their hides, wool, dairy products, and sometimes their services as soldiers and bodyguards. The ecological borders between pastoral societies and town-building populations were usually scenes of lively trade.

Because pastoral societies were mobile, not permanently settled, they expressed social relationships not so much in terms of where people lived but rather in terms of kinship, that is, who was related by "blood" to whom—closely, distantly, or not at all. They typically had a tribal organization, though this has nothing to do with how "advanced" or "primitive" they were. Rather, we define a tribe as a group whose members claim to be descended from a common ancestor. Usually, a tribe is typically the largest group in a region claiming shared descent. Tribes may also be divided into smaller groups of people who see themselves as relatively more closely related, from clans to lineages to nuclear families.

In the latter part of Big Era Three, we see emerging an important long-term and recurring pattern in history: encounters involving both peaceful exchanges and violent clashes between agrarian peoples and pastoral nomads of Inner Eurasia, the Sahara Desert, and other sectors of the Great Arid Zone. An early example is the far-reaching social and political change that occurred in the second and first millennia BCE when several different pastoral peoples of Inner Eurasia pressed into the agrarian, urbanized regions of Southwest Asia, India, and Europe, sometimes moving in peacefully, sometimes raiding, sometimes conquering.

Also, the mobility of pastoral societies and their vital interests in trade meant that they served to link different agrarian societies with one another and to encourage growth of long networks of commercial and cultural exchange. The best known of these networks is the Inner Eurasian silk roads, the series of trade routes that pastoral peoples dominated and that moved goods and ideas between China in the east and India, Southwest Asia, and the Mediterranean region to the west.

HUMANS AND IDEAS

It was in Big Era Two that Homo sapiens evolved its capacity for language. This wondrous skill meant that humans could engage in collective learning, not only sharing information and ideas from one community to another, sometimes across great distances, but also passing an ever-increasing stockpile of beliefs from one generation to the next.

In Big Era Three, world population started growing at a faster rate than ever before. The size and density of communities expanded, and networks of communication by land and sea became more extensive and sophisticated. Along with these developments came, as we might well expect, an intensification in the flow of information and a general speed-up in the accumulation of knowledge of all kinds.

One example is religious knowledge. In the early millennia of Big Era Three certain ideas, practices, and artistic expressions centered on the worship of female deities spread widely along routes of trade and migration to embrace a large part of western Eurasia. Another example is the idea and technology of writing, which emerged first, as far as we know, in either Egypt or Mesopotamia and spread widely from there to the eastern Mediterranean and India. A third example is the horse-drawn chariot, which may have first appeared in the Inner Eurasian steppes and within less than a thousand years spread all across Eurasia from western Europe to China.

> **Homo sapiens evolved its capacity for language... [we] could engage in collective learning, not only sharing information and ideas from one community to another... but also passing an ever-increasing stockpile of beliefs from one generation to the next.**

Complex Societies As Centers of Innovation

Since we are focusing here on large-scale changes in world history, we cannot discuss in detail the numerous scientific, technological, and cultural innovations that complex societies achieved in Big Era Three in Afroeurasia and, from the second millennium BCE, in Mesoamerica (Mexico and Central America) and South America.

To take just one early example, the city-dwellers of Sumer in southern Mesopotamia, which is as far as we know the earliest urban civilization, made fundamental scientific and technical breakthroughs in the fourth and third millennia BCE. Sometime before 3000 BCE, Sumerian scribes worked out a system of numerical notation in the writing script they used, called cuneiform. For computation they devised both base-ten (decimal) and base-sixty systems. The base-sixty method has endured in the ways we keep time and reckon the circumference of a circle—60 seconds to the minute, 60 minutes to the hour, and 360 degrees in the circumference of a circle. Sumerians used a combination of base-ten and base-sixty mathematics, together with a growing understanding of geometry, for everyday government and commerce, as well as to survey land, chart the stars, design buildings, and build irrigation works. Other technical innovations included the seed drill, the vaulted arch, refinements in bronze metallurgy, and, most ingenious of all, the wheel. This concept was probably first applied to pottery making, later to transport and plowing.

The cuneiform writing system used in ancient Mesopotamia and shown on this clay tablet combined logographic and phonetic elements.

Different Cultural Styles

Within complex societies, such as those that emerged in the great river valleys, the interchange of information and ideas tended to be so intense that each society developed a distinct cultural style. We can discern these distinctive styles today in the surviving remnants of buildings, art objects, written texts, tools, and other material remains.

We should, however, keep two ideas in mind. One is that all complex societies were invariably changing, rather than possessing timeless, static cultural traits. The style of a civilization changed from one generation to the next because cultural expressions and values were invariably bound up with the natural environment, economic life, and politics, which were continuously changing as well. The second point is that early civilizations were not culturally self-contained. All of them developed and changed as they did partly because of their connections to other societies near and far, connections that played themselves out in trade, migration, war, and cultural exchange.

CHAPTER 3 STUDY QUESTIONS

1. Domestication depended on both environmental conditions and human action. What conditions do you think had to be present in the environment to make the domestication of plants and animals possible?

2. Would the populations of early cities have become progressively more like one another or less like one another? Explain your choice. What factors might have favored the growth of social and cultural diversity in early cities? What types of evidence might reveal social and cultural diversity in cities? Do conditions in big cities today encourage greater or lesser diversity?

3. What features of city-living might have favored the development of writing, public laws, mathematics, or engineering technology? Which social classes do you think benefited most from these developments? Which social classes were least affected by them?

4. Compare the advantages and disadvantages of living as hunter-foragers with those of living as farmers, pastoral nomads, or city-dwelling workers. Given a choice among them, which of those four ways of life would you prefer? Explain your choice.

5. How would you describe the relationship in ancient times between city-dwellers and farmers on the one hand and pastoral nomads on the other? Where these relations predominantly peaceful or predominantly hostile? What advantages did each gain from peaceful exchange of goods?

CHAPTER 4

Big Era Four

Expanding Networks of Exchange and Encounter, 1200 BCE–500 CE

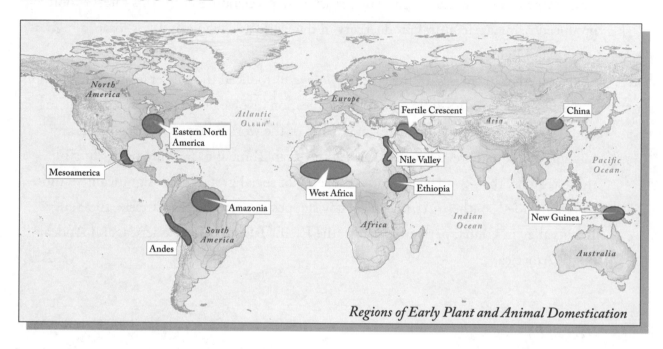

Regions of Early Plant and Animal Domestication

In Big Era Three, humans in several parts of the world began to produce food, adopt new forms of social organization, and interact more intensively with one another over longer distances than in any earlier times. In Big Era Four those patterns continued, though at a faster pace. World population continued to increase in the first millennium BCE, though it leveled off in the early centuries CE. More cities appeared. States, which first emerged in Big Era Three as a way of organizing large populations under a single governing authority, now appeared in new forms that were bigger, more complex, and more efficient at collecting taxes from the population.

Interregional systems of communication allowed goods, technologies, and ideas to move, sometimes thousands of miles. Interlocking networks of roads, trails, and sea lanes connected almost all parts of Afroeurasia and, in the Americas, extensive areas of Mesoamerica and the Andean mountain spine of South America. Among the ideas transmitted along these routes were new belief systems, which invited peoples of differing languages and cultural traditions to share common standards of morality and trust.

HUMANS AND THE ENVIRONMENT

We might argue that compared to today, when humans are expending huge amounts of energy to shape the physical and natural earth to their own purposes, Big Era Four was not a period of drastic environmental change. That, however, is a relative matter. If we compare that era to the three earlier ones, it is clear that humans were extracting energy from nature and from the earth's outer crust at an accelerating pace. This intervention produced rising agricultural productivity in the world as a whole and, for some, a higher standard of living.

Recall that in the essay on Big Era Two, we introduced the concepts of extensification and intensification. In Big Era Four, intensification involved human groups introducing both farming and pastoral nomadism in parts of the world where only foragers, if any humans at all, had previously lived. With the establishment of farming or herding in those regions, the size, density, and complexity of social groups grew significantly. Those places included southern Africa, the grassy steppes of northeastern Eurasia, the Yangzi River valley in China, parts of Oceania (the Pacific Islands), Mesoamerica, and Andean South America.

Technology

New tools and techniques that made those developments possible included improved hybrids of food crops and in Afroeurasia more extensive exploitation of horses and camels as work animals. Perhaps the single most important invention of the era was the technology of iron production. Beginning late in the second millennium BCE, people in both Southwest Asia and East Africa, independently of each other, acquired the knowledge of how to smelt iron and work it into useful objects. This technology rapidly spread across most of Afroeurasia.

Consequently, farmers wielding iron axes, hoes, spades, and plows opened millions of acres of virgin land. City artisans used iron hammers, chisels, and saws to erect great buildings of wood and stone. And monarchs increasingly armed soldiers with iron weapons and armor. In other respects, we cannot really argue that Big Era Four was a time of great technological change in the world as a whole. Many of the most fundamental inventions, such as the wheel, the technology of pottery-making, or the horse harness, had already appeared. And basic inventions did not necessarily spread worldwide. Iron metallurgy, for example, did not reach the Americas, Australia, or Oceania in this period.

Population Growth

One fundamental development closely linked to the expansion of agriculture was population growth. Between 1000 BCE and 1 CE, world population appears to have risen from about 120,000,000 to 250,000,000. The rate of growth also went up. Between 3000 and 1000 BCE, it took about 1,600 years for world populations to double. Between 1000 BCE and 1 CE the doubling time was less than 1,000 years.

One cause of human biological success in the first millennium BCE may have been that in regions where people regularly interacted with one another, they slowly built up shared immunities to infectious diseases. This would especially have happened in densely populated regions like Southwest Asia, northern India, or northern China. Stronger natural immunities reduced mortality from recurring epidemics, permitting populations to grow at a faster rate. However, if some new infectious malady entered a region from afar, a severe epidemic might break out and populations take a plunge.

> Stronger natural immunities reduced mortality from recurring epidemics, permitting populations to grow at a faster rate.

Environmental Impact: The Fate of Forests

As populations grew, so did their impact on the environment. Though the pace of deforestation in Big Era Four may have been minor compared to the twentieth century, it appears to have greatly accelerated compared to earlier times. Clearing forest cover for fuels, farming, or grazing meant that more people could live on a given area of land. Over the long run, however, forest cutting produced soil erosion, chronic shortages of wood fuel, periodic famines, and extinction of some local animal and plant species. Deforestation and the burning of trees, as well as wet rice farming, may even have begun to alter global climate.

We have sound archaeological evidence that in Big Era Four farmers cut or burned forests on a substantial scale in the Mediterranean basin, western Europe, East Africa, the Ganges River valley, China, and other regions. In Mesoamerica and the Andes Mountains, societies had neither iron tools nor large work animals until much later in history. In both those regions, however, land clearing proceeded steadily because those societies learned to deploy human muscle power on a large scale and very efficiently.

HUMANS AND OTHER HUMANS

The doubling of world numbers in Big Era Four, coupled with increasing density of farming populations, meant that in many places humans had no other choice but to experiment with new ways of organizing their social, economic, and cultural relations. For one thing, many more humans lived in cities at the end of this era than at the beginning.

This does not mean that anything close to a majority of people inhabited cities or that urban growth was steady and uninterrupted. Urban populations rose and fell. In fact, cities appeared and disappeared, in connection with regional or local changes in agricultural production, long-distance trade, infectious disease environments, political conditions, and other factors. The table below tells us something about the general patterns of global urbanization between 1200 BCE and 500 CE.[6]

Year	Number of largest cities	Size of largest cities	Total population of largest cities
BCE			
1200	16	24,000–50,000	499,000
650	20	30,000–120,000	894,000
430	51	30,000–200,000	2,877,000
CE			
100	75	30,000–450,000	5,181,000
500	47	40,000–400,000	3,892,000

Why do you think there were fewer large cities in the world in 500 CE than in 100 CE?

We can see here that urbanization rose steadily up to the second century CE, then declined in the following 400 years. We can definitely link the upswing to the appearance of several large states and empires, all of which accumulated sizable agricultural, mineral, and commercial wealth. The downswing after the second century CE may be partly connected to pandemic disease outbreaks, the decline of large empires, and extended economic recessions in the major agrarian regions.

> **Archaeologists studying the ancient Americas ... have pushed evidence (of) urbanization further and further back in time.**

The Multiplying of Cities

In Afroeurasia, cities grew and multiplied partly because they developed increasingly strong commercial ties with one another, sometimes across long distances. About 100 CE, the world's two biggest cities were almost certainly Rome, with a population nearing one million, and Luoyang in China's Han empire. The urban downswing that occurred from the third century CE was certainly related to the decline of the Han and Roman empires.

Most cities of Big Era Four were multifunctional, serving as centers of government, religion, trade, manufacturing, education, and artistic display. In some cities, such as Rome or Alexandria (in Egypt), all these functions operated simultaneously. Other cities had more specialized purposes, for example, towns of the Mediterranean coast or Inner Eurasia, which functioned chiefly to transship goods along routes of trade.

Archaeologists studying the ancient Americas in recent decades have pushed evidence urbanization further and further back in time. Along a thirty-mile stretch of the Peruvian coast known as Norte Chico, researchers have surveyed as many as thirty small cities, some of them founded no later than about 3200 BCE. The oldest of these centers predates the appearance of cities anywhere in the world except Sumer in Mesopotamia. The contours of a complex society governed by an aristocratic minority comes into clearer view at the ruins of Chavín de Huántar, a center for ritual practice and pilgrimage whose construction began around 800 BCE in the Andean highlands of northern Peru. The earliest city we know of in Mesoamerica emerged about 1350 BCE in the tropical lowlands that border the Gulf of Mexico. This center, known by its ruins as San Lorenzo, featured an artificial central platform 150 feet high and two-thirds of a mile on each side. This city and others that followed in the region developed in association with the early

A stretch of the Roman Empire's elaborate road network south of Rome.

Olmec (Olmeca) society. These centers may have been the earliest places in the Americas where an aristocratic minority exercised some type of permanent authority over the common population of farmers, artisans, and hunters. By 600 CE, the city of Teotihuacán in the Valley of Mexico (the region of modern Mexico City) may have had a population of more than 150,000, making it one of the top ten largest cities in the world at that time.

Giant Empires

States of unprecedented size arose in Big Era Four partly because of new technologies that permitted rulers to extend their systems of central command farther and farther away from their capitals. One of these advances was the perfecting of horse riding. All across Afroeurasia, armed cavalry, which could operate on almost any terrain, replaced chariots as an instrument of military conquest and control. Soldiers, as well as state messengers and envoys, could transmit political orders and vital news by horseback faster than any other way.

Other innovations that contributed to imperial growth were advanced road construction (the Persians and Romans), canal building (the Chinese), and the emergence of the dromedary camel as the principal transport animal in arid lands from Africa to northwest India.

Below is a table of the three biggest empires of the 1000 BCE to 500 CE period. Their land area is compared to that of the continental United States.[7]

State	Approximate year	Approximate size in square miles
Han empire	50 BCE	2,509,000
Achaemenid Persian empire	500 BCE	2,123,000
Roman empire	100 CE	1,698,400
Continental United States	Present	3,021,296

These ancient states were empires not only because they were big but also because a single government, and an elite class of particular origin (Han Chinese, Indo-Iranian-speaking Persians, Latin-speaking Romans), ruled over peoples of diverse linguistic, ethnic, and religious identities.

In Big Era Four, the majority of the world's people probably did not live within the frontiers of empires. Some lived in city-states, which were relatively small sovereign territories centered on a single city. Greek and Phoenician city-states of the Mediterranean are obvious examples. Many other people lived under no state authority but in societies organized in kinship groups.

Nevertheless, a sweeping view of Afroeurasia at about 100 CE reveals a nearly continuous chain of states, most of them gigantic, extending from the Atlantic to the Pacific. All these states enjoyed extended periods of political order and economic prosperity, and those conditions in turn stimulated long-distance exchanges of products and ideas, not just within states but between one another.

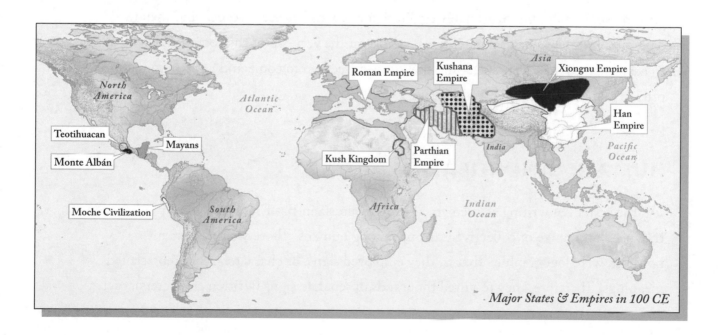

Major States & Empires in 100 CE

In Big Era Four, especially between about 300 BCE and 300 CE, merchants, shippers, camel drivers, and sea captains extended and strengthened trade routes across Inner Eurasia on the silk roads, the basins of the Mediterranean and Black seas, and the Indian Ocean. And the last centuries of the era also saw the beginnings of camel caravan trade across the Sahara, linking peoples of tropical Africa to the Mediterranean rim.

The Shape of Societies

In Big Era Four the vast majority of the world's population were farmers, herders, or foragers. They subsisted on their own production, and they lived short lives compared to today. However, more and bigger cities, plus the rise of states that concentrated immense amounts of wealth, led to sharper distinctions of social class between elite minorities that held wealth, power, and privilege, and everyone else. In urban societies there might have also been a sizeable class of merchants, artisans, scholars, and other people with special skills who accumulated substantial wealth, though not necessarily much political power or privilege.

At the bottom of the social scale were slaves. There is no doubt that this era witnessed a huge expansion of slavery and organized slave trade in many parts of the world, notably the Mediterranean basin. For example, the slave population in the central part of the Roman empire at the end of the first century BCE may have been as much as 40 percent of the total population.

In all the urbanized societies of Big Era Four, adult males dominated political and social life, as far as we know. One would have to visit forager, pastoral, or small-scale farming societies to find reasonably egalitarian relations between women and men in daily life. In the big states and empires, women at the very top of the social ladder appear to have enjoyed, relatively speaking, the greatest freedom to come and go, accumulate property, and influence political affairs.

HUMANS AND IDEAS

The system of writing that emerged in Afroeurasia in Big Era Three greatly enhanced the speed and range of collective learning among humans. Those writing systems, however, were logographic. That is, they employed signs, or characters, that represented meanings. Therefore, they required thousands of separate signs (written characters), each having a specific meaning. This kind of writing system had the advantage of allowing people to express meanings in very precise, subtle ways.

The new development in Big Era Four, however, was the appearance of the earliest alphabetic writing systems. The signs used in them represented, for the most part, sounds of speech, not meanings. Meanings may be expressed in millions of ways, but the number of sounds humans can make with their lips and tongues is drastically limited. Alphabetic systems, therefore, relied on a small number of signs (for example, 26 in the English alphabet, 28 in the Arabic one). Nevertheless, these signs could be arranged in countless ways to represent the nuances of human thought.

The earliest alphabetic system that we know of appeared in Southwest Asia near the end of the second millennium BCE. In the following centuries variations of that system spread from the Mediterranean basin to India. People could master alphabetic systems faster and easier than logographic ones. Therefore literacy spread rapidly in Big Era Four, though especially among scholars, priests, officials, and merchants, not ordinary farmers and workers. Nor did alphabetic systems completely replace logographic ones. The Chinese character-based system is the leading case of modern logographic writing.

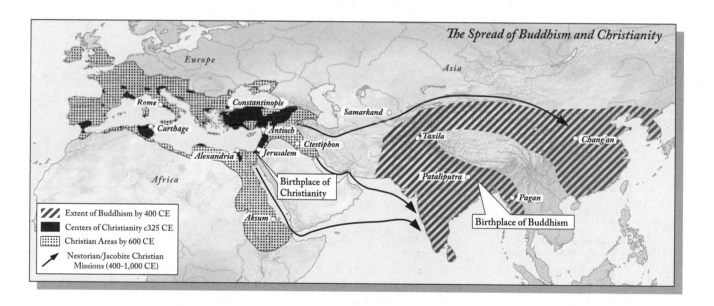

Big Religions

Another development of Big Era Four, and one related to the spread of writing, was the appearance of several belief systems that embraced people of differing languages and cultural traditions, what we often call "world religions." The great majority of people in that era practiced local religions, that is, systems that centered on local gods and goddesses, sacred places in nature, astrology, magic, and pronouncements of shamans—individuals who mediated between the natural and supernatural worlds. In large states and empires, religious life tended to be diverse, though rulers could seldom resist encouraging their subjects to think of them as individuals with supernatural powers or even as divine beings. For example, when the Roman state made the transition from a republic to a sprawling autocratic empire, its leaders were transformed from ordinary mortals into gods.

Since people do not appear to have lacked for religious life on a local scale from very early times, why did several large-scale belief systems emerge in Big Era Four? In fact, why did all the major world religions appear in that era, with the exception of Islam? One possibility is that by about the middle of the first millennium BCE, Afroeurasia reached a level of population and an intensity of commercial and cultural interchange that required larger systems of morality and shared belief. The new religious systems provided foundations of cultural communication, moral expectation, and personal trust among people who were meeting, sharing ideas, and doing business with one another far beyond their local neighborhoods. The new belief systems, however, were by no means all the same. Each one offered distinctive answers to persistent questions about the human condition and different ways of approaching worship, ritual, and communal life. The table below provides some basic information about new religions that appeared in Big Era Four.

Belief system	Time of appearance	Homeland
Buddhism	5th century BCE	Northern India
Christianity	1st century CE	Southwest Asia
Confucianism	5th century BCE	Northern China
Daoism (Taoism)	5th century BCE	Northern China
Hinduism	early 1st millennium BCE	Northern India
Judaism	early 1st millennium BCE	Southwest Asia

In addition to these six, what other belief systems might be added to this list?

Buddhism, Christianity, Hinduism, Judaism, and Daoism all offered paths to self-transformation and to eternal salvation in one form or another. Christianity and Judaism were the most firmly monotheistic, proclaiming one omnipotent and omniscient god. Hinduism made room for numerous, powerful gods and goddesses. Buddhism and Daoism also accepted the existence of multiple divine beings in various forms and incarnations. Like Christianity and Judaism, however, Buddhism, Daoism, and Hinduism envisioned a unitary, all-encompassing cosmic reality.

Buddhism and Christianity emphasized their universalism and appeal to all humans, and both spread widely across ethnic and linguistic frontiers. Judaism remained closely identified with the Hebrew people and their descendants, though by the end of Big Era Four a diaspora of Jewish communities extended nearly across Afroeurasia. All six systems taught that human relations should be guided by kindness, selflessness, and decency. Confucianism, which some scholars characterize as an ethical system rather than a religion, particularly emphasized public moral behavior, good government, and social responsibility.

These six systems may of course be compared and contrasted in numerous other ways. In terms of general beliefs and practices, none can be set rigidly apart from all the others. Also, within each tradition, significant variations developed depending on local cultural tendencies and social environments. For example, in the Christian tradition, several different "churches," each with distinctive beliefs and practices, emerged during the first or early second millennium CE. These included the Eastern (Greek) Orthodox, Roman Catholic, Arian, Nestorian, and Ethiopian churches. In Afroeurasia the only major belief system that did not appear in Big Era Four was Islam, which came on the scene in the seventh century CE.

Philosophy

All these belief systems had philosophical aspects in the sense that they encouraged investigations into the structure and meaning of the physical and natural universe. None of them was incompatible with types of inquiry and speculation that we associate with the beginnings of science. In the Aegean Sea region, for example, Greek-speaking scholars, whose religion in the first millennium BCE embraced a large household of deities, developed a method of scientific and moral questioning known as natural philosophy. According to Hellenism, the system of thought and creativity based on Greek language and culture, human reason could be applied to developing general theories to explain natural, cosmic, and psychological phenomena. These thinkers saw no contradiction between efforts to detect universal patterns in nature and their conviction that the gods fundamentally ruled it.

CHAPTER 4 STUDY QUESTIONS

1. What factors promoted contact between different peoples and societies in Big Era Four? What factors promoted particular peoples and societies to develop shared culture and identity?

2. How might you relate such factors as increased urbanization, more complex trade, alphabetic writing, and larger empires to the rise of large-scale religions?

3. How did new agricultural technologies that appeared in Big Era Four illustrate the ideas of "extensification" and "intensification" introduced in Chapter 2?

4. What factors contributed to the increase in long-distance trade in Big Era Four?

5. How did rulers come to have greater control over their subjects in this Big Era than they had in earlier times? Do you think this control benefited the elite classes only, or did it benefit common men and women as well? Explain your choice.

CHAPTER 5

Big Era Five

Patterns of Interregional Unity, 300–1500 CE

For more than five millennia the population of Afroeurasia had grown steadily, forming larger and more complex political units such as the Han Chinese, Persian Achaemenid, and Roman empires. Around 300 to 400 CE this cycle of empire building came nearly to a halt, and even for a time reversed itself. The ancient world came to an end, and over the 1200 years of Big Era Five, many elements of the modern world first came into view. In this essay we examine some of the dynamics at work, and explore their significance.

One distinguishing feature of this era was its unusual demographic (population) history. Overall there were fluctuations with a long-term upward trend, culminating with a significant rise at the end of the period to 400 million people globally. This number broke the ceiling on growth that had limited the population advances of earlier agrarian societies. The population surge of Big Era Five was linked to the spread of innovations in agriculture, especially numerous small changes to improve irrigation, domestic animal breeds, and enrichment of the soil. These advances, which took place from Europe and West Africa to China and Japan, increased the number of people that a given acre of land could feed. Long-distance trade also supplied people with a more varied diet and numerous products that at least marginally improved the quality of life.

Politically, Big Era Five was marked by the founding of a kaleidoscope of city-states, kingdoms, and empires. For the first time large empires appeared in West Africa, Mesoamerica, and South America. States and the economic systems linked to them became more complex. A few empires emerged that were even bigger than the Han and Roman states of Big Era Four. The largest of these were the Arab Muslim empire of the eighth century and the Mongol empire of the thirteenth century.

Long-distance commerce grew and cities multiplied across Afroeurasia, especially between 1000 and 1500 CE. Big Era Five saw the emergence of the Indian Ocean basin as a new focus of busy economic interchange. Notably during the era of the Mongol empire and the several big Mongol states that followed it, the silk roads across Afroeurasia bustled with caravan trade in silks, cottons, spices, tea, horses, ceramic wares, and numerous other products. Caravans and ships also carried ideas; during this era, a great deal of scientific and technological cross-fertilization took place, especially in Afroeurasia but also in the Americas. In America, artistic and architectural techniques and styles spread from the Olmec city-states of the second and first millennium BCE far and wide across Mesoamerica and to Native American peoples farther north.

Culturally, Big Era Five featured the consolidation of several belief systems and the continuing retreat of the purely local religions of farmers, foragers, and pastoral nomads. The number of distinct religious traditions in the world almost certainly declined significantly, even as universalist religions, that is, those that appealed to people across boundaries of language and local culture, grew by leaps and bounds. Islam, the last of the major world belief systems, emerged in the seventh century CE. Islam, together with Christianity and Buddhism, offered a universal message of comfort, moral living, and salvation that gave them widespread appeal.

> Not all individuals and societies benefited equally—or benefited at all—from these trends in political, economic, and cultural growth. Millions fell victim to conquests, millions more paid heavy taxes to authoritarian rulers, and slavery continued to thrive.

Not all individuals and societies benefited equally—or benefited at all—from these trends in political, economic, and cultural growth. Millions fell victim to conquests, millions more paid heavy taxes to authoritarian rulers, and slavery continued to thrive. Nevertheless, an array of ingenious technological advances allowed humankind to feed, clothe, and shelter itself even as global population grew faster than in any earlier era.

HUMANS AND THE ENVIRONMENT

Big Era Five began with a sharp population decline that lasted from the third to the sixth centuries CE and that affected large areas of Afroeurasia. We do not entirely understand why this demographic downturn occurred, but it is likely associated with a number of factors. One was a cycle of climatic change that produced drier conditions

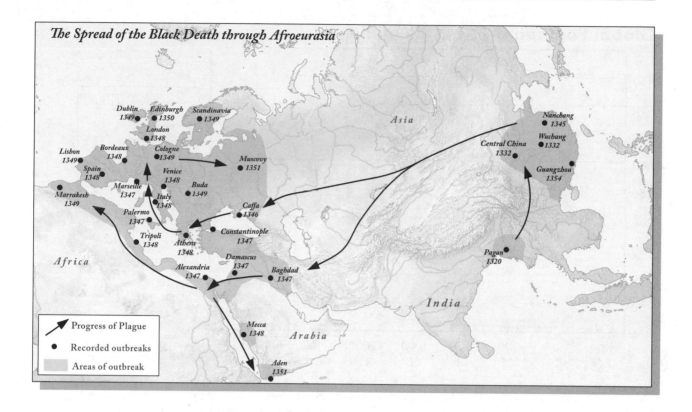

The Spread of the Black Death through Afroeurasia

and consequently declines in agricultural productivity, notably in irrigated river valleys. Another was outbreaks of infectious disease epidemics. The one that hit the Mediterranean region in the sixth century is known as Justinian's Plague after the famous Roman emperor of that period. Economic recession and epidemics disrupted established empires and states across Afroeurasia, and this helped open agrarian societies to recurring invasions and migrations of pastoral nomadic peoples from the Inner Eurasian steppes.

By the sixth century CE, however, the overall population of Afroeurasia started to rise again. But this time it kept on going for more than 700 years. By around 1250 CE global population reached about 235 million. Then, in the early fourteenth century, a series of hemispheric-wide disease epidemics, especially the Black Death of mid-century, intervened to reduce the population of Eurasia and North Africa by a quarter to a third. The onset of a cycle of lower temperatures in the Northern Hemisphere, what historians call the Little Ice Age, also contributed to agricultural depression and declining population, especially in Europe, Russia, and China, and probably also in North America. This demographic setback, however, did not last long. By 1500 world population had surpassed all previous levels, reaching 400 million.[8]

Global Population Trend (in millions)

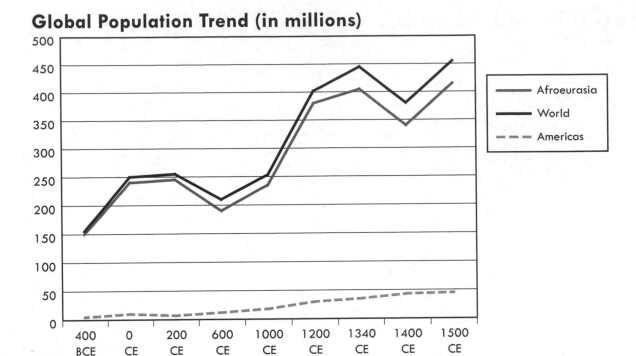

Why do you think the population of Afroeurasia temporarily dipped between the third and sixth centuries CE and again in the 14th century CE? Why did the population of the Americas maintain a steady rise during these periods?

Population, Agriculture, and Trade

Why did world population start moving up faster toward the end of Big Era Five? One factor is that continuing improvements in farming technology increased the productivity of the land, allowing food supplies to run ahead of population growth. By 1500 CE, states and empires were able to feed and clothe more people, build larger armies, and accumulate much more tax revenue to enhance their power. Better agriculture evolved from centuries of identifying the best techniques, seeds, and strategies of farming in particular regions from which these ideas spread across Afroeurasia by the trade routes. In northern Europe, for example, the moldboard plow and the horse collar were inventions that enabled European peasants to cultivate heavy wet soils and open immense new areas to farming. This led to significant population increases. In India, the opening of the vast delta of the Ganges valley to rice cultivation allowed large population growth in Bengal. Similar patterns of improvement can be seen in the Americas. For example, expertise in breeding and growing corn, beans, and squash first developed under the Olmecs, then spread throughout much of North America, sustaining towns, cities, and empires.

More intensive commercial exchange and movements of peoples across Afroeurasia by land and sea during Big Era Five also helped stimulate population growth. On land, the rise of great empires that originated among pastoral peoples—the Huns, Arabs, Turks, and Mongols—was made possible by technological developments that enabled these peoples to better exploit the steppe and desert lands they inhabited. In the area of transport and war-making, these advances included the invention of the stirrup and the North Arabian camel saddle, which made riding on horses or camels a much more stable experience. For more than a millennium, pastoralists, especially Turkish-speaking horse nomads and Arabic-speaking camel nomads, were the world leaders in mounted warfare.

> **In spite of these long trends of growth in population, production, and trade, all parts of the world remained susceptible to war, flood, famine, and disease, events that could suddenly interrupt a trend of economic and population growth.**

(The Americas had neither horses nor camels until after 1500 CE.) The rise of pastoral power was accompanied by increased volume and complexity of trade across Afroeurasia's Great Arid Zone, the belt of dry country that extends from western Africa to northern China. Also in this era, the trans-Saharan trade in gold, salt, and other commodities stimulated growth of population and cities north and south of the desert, as well as cultural exchange, notably the Islamic faith, between the Mediterranean lands and West Africa.

In the seas of Afroeurasia from the Mediterranean to the China seas, new ship construction, sailing, and navigational techniques greatly stimulated the circulation of goods, people, and ideas across maritime Eurasia. Key inventions included the compass, the stern post ship rudder, the astrolabe, and the fore-and-aft, triangle-shaped lateen sail. The techniques of banking and business organization also became more

Astrolabe attributed to Ahmad ibn Muhammad al-Naqqash, dated to Zaragoza, Spain in the eleventh century CE.

Saluator dicens summo pontifici Tu suppler ora.
Imperatori Tu protege. Rustico Tuqz labora

Tu suppler ora

Tu protege

Tuqz labora

German illustration of the three estates of medieval society, with peasants making up the lowest third. Who is the figure in the center of the picture, and why is this figure included?

sophisticated. By 1500, the societies of both island Southeast Asia and coastal East Africa were becoming increasingly integrated into the wider Afroeurasian intercommunicating zone. The Indian Ocean emerged as a major new arena of world trade to rival the Mediterranean.

In spite of these long trends of growth in population, production, and trade, all parts of the world remained susceptible to war, flood, famine, and disease, events that could suddenly interrupt a trend of economic and population growth. If farmers and herders stopped producing more because of some unforeseen crisis, then population growth came to a halt or numbers even went down, as the era of the Black Death grimly demonstrated. We should remember that human beings still depended on the energy of the sun, with a little help from windmills, water wheels, and sail craft, to produce all food, textiles, and other products. The "fossil fuel revolution," which unleashed the vast energy power of coal, petroleum, and natural gas, lay several centuries in the future.

Environmental Problems

Amid the growth and prosperity of Big Era Five, there was also a strong countercurrent: a sharp global increase in environmental degradation. Historians have documented the environmental impact of state-building, urbanization, and commercial expansion on the Byzantine empire, the Muslim empires of Southwest Asia and North Africa, and the empires of South and East Asia. In particular, deforestation increased, provoking long-term soil erosion and frequent flooding. There were also growing wood shortages owing to the accelerating demand for wood energy for domestic fires, brewing, dyeing, metallurgy, and other industrial uses, as well as dependence upon wood as the primary material for constructing buildings and ships. For example, at the start of Big Era

Five, forest clearing in Roman Italy caused irreversible soil degradation and contributed to serious food shortages. In China, deforestation that accompanied urbanization and economic expansion contributed to river flooding, which devastated villages and farmlands. The incidence of flooding on China's major rivers appears to have increased steadily in Big Era Five.

> **Advances in agriculture and commerce enabled humans to push beyond previous population levels and to bring more regions into sustained contact with one another.**

Despite important fluctuations in this period, by 1500 CE populations had clearly surpassed previous levels around the world. Advances in agriculture and commerce enabled humans to push beyond previous population levels and to bring more regions into sustained contact with one another.

HUMANS AND OTHER HUMANS

Big Era Five marks the apex of pastoral power across Afroeurasia. Since Big Era Four, pastoral nomads had constituted a serious challenge to settled societies and agrarian empires across the region. Beginning in the fourth century CE, armed invasions perpetrated by Uighurs, Huns, Arabs, and other mounted armies, plus the spread of epidemic disease, seriously weakened several agrarian empires. The western Roman empire totally collapsed. A recovery then ensued. The period starting in the fifth century CE witnessed the rise of the Gupta empire in India, the Arab empires in west central Afroeurasia, and the Tang and Sung empires in China. These states were undermined, however, by the eleventh or twelfth centuries owing to large-scale Turkic and Mongol migrations. The Mongol conquest from 1206 to 1260 created an empire that stretched from Korea to eastern Europe. Under Chingis Khan (Genghis Khan) and his successors, the Mongol state at its height around 1260 controlled a territory of close to 7 million square miles, making it the largest empire in human history.

In Europe, the Byzantine empire and the early Russian empire came to flower in Big Era Five, while in Africa south of the Sahara a number of important states emerged, among them Ghana and Mali in West Africa and Great Zimbabwe in southern

Africa. From about the seventh century, city-states whose merchant populations were predominantly Muslim flourished along the East African coast, shipping gold, ivory, and numerous other products to the wider Indian Ocean world. In Southeast Asia, several maritime empires emerged, for example, Srivijaya and Majapahit, which drew great wealth from trade in spices. In the Americas, the Aztec and Incan territorial empires, which emerged late in this era, bear comparison to those of Afroeurasia.

The comparisons below show the remarkable scale of the Arab Muslim and Mongol states. On the other hand, neither state lasted as a unified empire more than about half a century. The outer areas of the Arab Muslim empire soon broke away from the central lands. In the Mongol case, Chingis Khan's sons and grandsons launched wars against one another within about thirty years of the great conqueror's death. Those struggles led to the dismemberment of the realm into four Mongol-ruled monarchies.[9]

State	Approximate Year	Approximate size in square miles
Roman empire	100 CE	1,698,000
Arab Muslim empire	750 CE	4,246,000
Sung empire (China)	1000 CE	1,158,000
Mongol empire	1250 CE	6,948,000
Inca empire (Andes Mts.)	1500 CE	772,000
Continental United States	present	3,021,000

The Scale of Warfare

In Big Era Five, warfare reached new levels of violence, thanks to the widespread use of projectile weapons, such as the catapult, the long bow, the compound bow, and the crossbow. Chinese armies first deployed gunpowder weapons in the form of primitive cannons and muskets, but firearms soon spread to India, West Asia, the Mediterranean, and West Africa, and the technology continually improved. The ability to organize large armies linking cavalry and infantry in complex formations became developed further as well. The pastoral Arabs in the seventh and eighth centuries and the Mongols in the thirteenth century learned to combine cavalry warfare with the military techniques of agrarian empires, for example, the use of catapults and other siege weapons to breach the walls of cities.

In the seas of Afroeurasia, naval warfare did not drastically change throughout most of this era. In the Mediterranean, sea battles featured clashes between large galleys rowed by dozens of oarsmen. But there were signs of change. Both the Byzantines and the Arabs started using "Greek fire," a petroleum-based substance, in naval encounters. More importantly, dramatic changes occurred in the navigation of the world's oceans. The widespread adoption of the compass and the stern post rudder increased the range and reliability of sailing along Afroeurasia's chain of seas. For example, colossal Chinese sailing vessels capable of carrying hundreds of sailors, merchants, and travelers over long distances appeared after 1000 CE. When the Chinese admiral Zheng-He visited Southeast Asia, India, Sri Lanka, the Persian Gulf, and the East African coast between 1405 and 1433, he had several ships that were 400 feet or more long and had five or more masts.

> **Growth in production and commerce also stimulated more urbanization in both Afroeurasia and the Americas. By 1500, more humans lived in cities than ever before.**

In the northwestern Atlantic a completely different tradition of naval construction emerged by the fifteenth century. It brought together the fixed square sails of Mediterranean galleys and the triangular lateen sails of Arab feluccas and dhows. This rigging, together with stout hulls designed for the rough wind and sea conditions of the north Atlantic, led to the development of the caravel, the first proper ocean-going ship. By 1460, Portuguese and Spanish mariners had reconnoitered the western coast of Africa and discovered the Canary Islands. By the same date, Basque and French fishermen had pioneered new cod fishing grounds off the coast of Labrador and Newfoundland. Christopher Columbus drew heavily on the lore of these earlier mariners in planning westward the voyages that took him and his crew, not to East Asia as intended, but to the islands of the Caribbean.

The Web of Commerce

Despite the Mongol conquests and the Black Death in the thirteenth and fourteenth centuries, Afroeurasia experienced a general trend of economic growth from about 700 to 1500. China and India emerged as major manufacturing centers, their silks, porcelain china, and cotton fabrics circulating as far as East Africa and northern Europe. Southwest Asia, whose population became predominantly Muslim in the centuries after 700, served as the turnstile of the hemisphere. Its cities generated finished goods, and its bazaars and warehouses transshipped goods in large quantities from one part of the hemisphere to the other. Merchants traded over long distances both in manufactures and precious commodities—gold, gemstones, spices, silks, porcelain, glassware, ivory—and bulk products—grain, metal ore, fish, timber, bolts of textiles. This trade stimulated production in all regions that had tradable resources, and it tightened economic relationships among Afroeurasia's far-flung regions.

As commerce grew, peoples of Japan, island Southeast Asia, equatorial Africa, and far northern Europe became increasingly linked into its web. For example, the state known as Great Zimbabwe rose to power in the savannas of southern Africa in the thirteenth century. Its prosperity derived partly from the sale of locally mined gold to merchants on the Indian Ocean coast, who traded this scarce commodity far and wide.

Growth in production and commerce also stimulated more urbanization in both Afroeurasia and the Americas. By 1500, more humans lived in cities than ever before. There were more cities with populations of 200,000 or more, including Florence, Tenochtitlán, Istanbul, Delhi, and Cairo. The mega-city of them all was Hangzhou, with a population that exceeded one million.

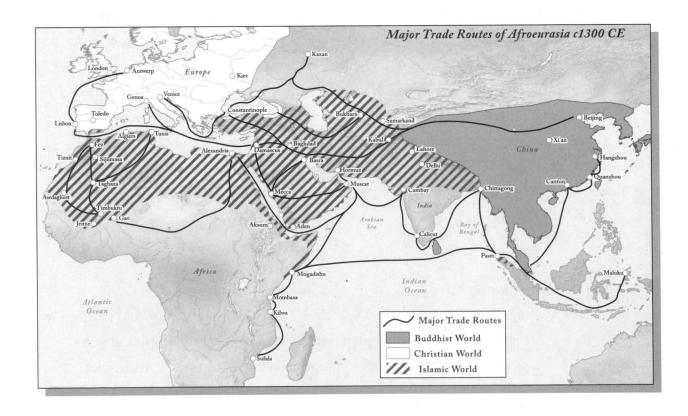

The Great Enclosure at Great Zimbabwe in southern Africa dates from the thirteenth to fifteenth centuries CE. What social, political, or cultural characteristics might we infer about Zimbabwe society from the size of this circular wall and its intricate stonework?

Understanding how extensive and sophisticated the trans-Afroeurasian exchange network had become by 1500 offers a fresh perspective on the next era, when Columbus and other intrepid mariners sailed across the Atlantic and Pacific oceans and around the Cape of Good Hope. When viewed against the background of steadily accumulating advances in transport and navigation and the thickening web of trade that crisscrossed Afroeurasia, it was almost certain that ocean-going mariners would eventually stumble upon the Americas.

HUMANS AND IDEAS

Two major cultural developments shaped Big Era Five. One was the consolidation of major belief systems, notably the rise and spread of the universalist religions of Christianity, Buddhism, and Islam. The other was the consolidation of scientific and technological traditions within particular complex societies and the diffusion of many new inventions and ideas across Afroeurasia.

Major Belief Systems

Among belief systems, Hellenism, that is, philosophical and scientific ideas expressed in the ancient Greek language, came to maturity in the first half of this era and spread widely. Hellenism provided an intellectual basis for applying human reasoning power to the problem of explaining nature and the cosmos. From about 500 BCE, Hellenistic

The Roman Catholic Cathedral in Durham, England (at right). Construction of this Norman Romanesque church began in 1087 CE. Below, the Great Buddha carving in the Longmen caves in China dates from 672 CE..

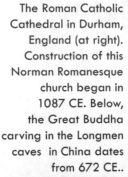

thought deeply influenced intellectual and artistic life throughout the Mediterranean world, Southwest Asia, India, and Inner Eurasia. Starting in the eighth century, Muslim, Jewish, and Christian scholars in Baghdad and other Southwest Asian cities developed a new body of ideas, notably in mathematics, astronomy, philosophy, and medicine that synthesized and built upon Hellenistic, Persian, Mesopotamian, and Indian knowledge. In the later centuries of the era, European scholars adopted much of this Muslim synthesis and reconciled Hellenistic and Christian understandings of nature.

The monotheistic religious traditions originating in Southwest Asia also developed and spread. Jewish monotheism, law, and ritual gradually linked dispersed Jewish communities all the way from the western Mediterranean to Inner Eurasia. Judaism was not a missionary religion but restricted to people born of Jewish mothers. The example of Jewish monotheism, however, laid spiritual and moral foundations for both Christianity and Islam.

Christianity became dominant on the northern shores of the Mediterranean and throughout Europe during Big Era Five. By 1500, it became an important minority faith in Southwest Asia, Egypt, and Ethiopia as well as in parts of Inner Eurasia and Russia. The medieval Christian church in western Europe was headed by the Pope in Rome and linked under a hierarchy of bishops, priests, monks, and nuns. The Greek Patriarch in Constantinople presided over the branch of the Christian tradition known as Greek, or Eastern Orthodoxy. These two rival Christian churches split permanently in 1054 CE.

In South Asia, Hinduism and Buddhism offered people possibilities of achieving one version or another of immortality, either through reincarnation, as in Hinduism and some forms of Buddhism, or through ethical devotion and right behavior. In East Asia, Confucianism stressed ethical righteousness, good government, and well-ordered society, while Daoism, and eventually Buddhism, emphasized the individual's quest for spiritual enlightenment. In the early centuries of the era, Christianity and Buddhism emerged as universalist religions, actively seeking to proclaim their message to all in the world who would listen, regardless of their ethnicity, language, or social status.

Hinduism, which experienced a great resurgence in India relative to Buddhism during the Gupta empire of the fourth and fifth centuries, continued to be closely associated with Indian society and culture. It also enjoyed favor among some ruling groups in Southeast Asia. Similarly, the Daoist and Confucian belief systems remained deeply rooted in China but also developed influence in Korea and Vietnam. In China beginning with

> **In South Asia, Hinduism and Buddhism offered people possibilities of achieving one version or another of immortality, either through reincarnation, as in Hinduism and some forms of Buddhism, or through ethical devotion and right behavior.**

the Tang dynasty in the sixth century, the path to careers in scholarship and government was the imperial examination system, which rewarded those who demonstrated intricate knowledge of Confucian ethics and statecraft. While Buddhism declined in India, the land of its birth, it spread from India to China, Korea, Japan, and mainland Southeast Asia.

Islam in the Tradition of Monotheism

The emergence of Islam as a third universalist religion was the most dramatic development of this era. Islam was monotheistic, and it had a scripture (the Qur'an) and a Prophet (Muhammad). It preached the unity of God and the need to conform one's behavior to God's will, or risk eternal damnation. Like Christianity and Buddhism, but unlike Judaism, Islam was a missionary religion that by 1500 had spread outward from the Arabian Peninsula to India, Southeast Asia,

> **The emergence of Islam as a third universalist religion was the most dramatic development of this era.**

China, Africa, and southern Europe. Under the early Muslim empires, especially the Abbasid dynasty (750–945) based in Baghdad, the caliphs, or rulers, drew heavily on the governing traditions of the Persian and Byzantine empires that preceded them. This included Hellenistic thought as well as the cultural heritage of India and Persia.

> **It is significant that all the major religions of the era tended to thrive in and around cities and to spread along the major trade routes.**

In the tenth century, Turkic-speaking pastoralists of Inner Eurasia converted to Islam, giving Muslim societies a new vitality. After 1000 CE, Turkic warriors invaded and founded governments in all the territories between Egypt and northern India. In the early fourteenth century, Turkic horse soldiers laid the foundations of the Ottoman state, which became a major new eastern Mediterranean empire within a hundred years. The conversion to Islam of Berber-speaking pastoralists in North Africa and the Sahara in roughly the same period led to the founding of new Muslim states that stretched into Spain.

It is significant that all the major religions of the era tended to thrive in and around cities and to spread along the major trade routes. This happened partly because organized religion tended to be closely linked with and supported by central governments, including large empires. Meanwhile, far from big cities and trade routes, people continued to

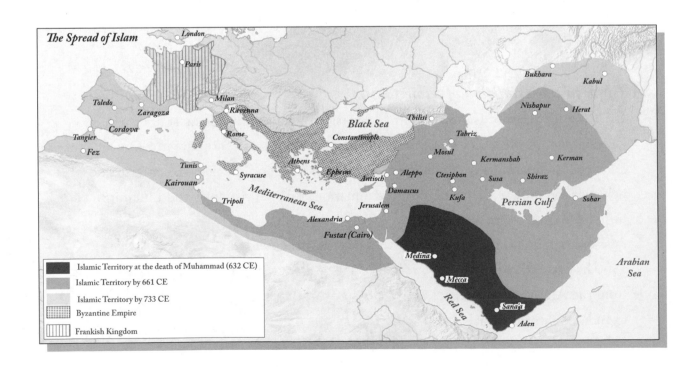

The Spread of Islam

- Islamic Territory at the death of Muhammad (632 CE)
- Islamic Territory by 661 CE
- Islamic Territory by 733 CE
- Byzantine Empire
- Frankish Kingdom

practice local religions that often involved worship of gods and spirits associated with nature.

In Big Era Five, indigenous religions in the Americas gradually coalesced into a smaller number of cultural traditions. By the eve of the Spanish conquests in the Americas, the Maya and Aztecs in Mesoamerica and the Inca in South America had created large imperial religions that were in some respects comparable to those of Afroeurasia. In North America and in South America, other than in the Andes, more localized religious traditions were the rule.

A copy of the Buddhist text called the Pure Light Dharani Sutra. It dates from between 690 and 704 CE, when the Silla dynasty ruled Korea. It is an early piece of woodblock printing, in which individual sheets of paper were pressed into wooden blocks with text and illustrations carved into them, and ink applied.

Science, Technology, and Learning

The second major cultural development of this era was the diffusion of scientific and technological ideas along the land and sea trade routes. By 1500, scientific ideas and technological devices, such as writing systems, mathematics, celestial observation, water management, navigation, and mining were widely available among interconnected societies. For example, mathematics and astronomy became an area for broad interchange of ideas and techniques. The abacus and other counting techniques spread broadly around Afroeurasia. The mathematical concepts of zero, the base-ten numerical system, and use of the decimal point for positional notation spread from Buddhist learning centers in India, where they were developed about the fourth century, to Southwest Asia, North Africa, Europe, and China. Innovations like these provided the basis for arithmetic, advanced mathematics, and the calculations of the movements of celestial bodies as the modern era approached. Archaeological evidence has also given us glimpses of the sophisticated mathematics and astronomy of Mesoamerican thinkers, notably in the Maya city-states.

Paper, the printing press, and movable type all developed first in either China or Korea, and then spread along the silk roads to South Asia, Europe, Southwest Asia, and Muslim Africa. Although the Chinese writing system remained dominant in East Asia, Arabic, Cyrillic (Greek Orthodox), and Latin alphabets became the bases for important new print languages. We can look to the Muslim and Christian European worlds for the early foundations of the modern university as a place where teachers and students came together to study, work, and live as an intellectual community. The college as a distinctive institution of scholars and students first developed in Muslim lands after 1000 CE and spread from there to Europe.

These two buildings are part of centers of higher learning dating to the fourteenth century CE. At top is the courtyard of the Attarin College, which was built in Fez, Morocco. At bottom is the Old Court of Corpus Christi College built in Cambridge, England. Both colleges, one serving Muslim, the other Catholic professors and students, were institutions within universities that had several colleges. How might you imagine the daily life of a young man living and studying in either of these colleges?

CHAPTER 5 STUDY QUESTIONS

1. If you were looking for the origins of the modern world in Big Era Five, what economic, technological, political, or intellectual evidence might you find that the world was becoming "modern"? What argument might you make that the world was not yet becoming modern? How would you define "modern" and "modernity?" (Look ahead to Chapter 7 for ideas.)

2. The infectious disease pandemic known as the Black Death wiped out up to a third of the population of Europe and the Mediterranean region within a short period in the fourteenth century. What factors do you think contributed to such huge population loss? What were some of the short-term economic and social effects of the Black Death? How do you think a comparable pandemic today would affect the way we live?

3. Why do you think that many local religions declined in this Big Era, while Christianity, Islam, and Buddhism spread widely and attracted millions of new adherents?

4. What technological factors, including military technology, contributed to the great success of Mongol conquests and empire-building in the thirteenth century?

5. Compare the reasons for and extent of global deforestation in Big Eras Four and Five. How would you account for the differences?

CHAPTER 6

Big Era Six

The Great Global Convergence, 1400–1800 CE

At the level of the human species as a whole, the most striking aspect of the period from 1400 to 1800 was the enormous extension of networks of communication and exchange that linked individuals and societies more and more tightly. Every region of the world became intricately connected to every other region, a development that we call the Great Global Convergence. Also in this era the world's population began to move dramatically upward, breaking through the ceilings on growth that had previously governed human affairs. Big Era Six saw striking changes in human history. Five key transformations mark the era:

First, human societies and the networks that connected them became much more complex. The most dramatic example of this is that for the first time in history, peoples of Afroeurasia began to interact on a large scale with peoples of the Americas (from the early sixteenth century) and Australasia (from the later eighteenth century).

A second major development was the Columbian Exchange of plants, animals, and microorganisms between Afroeurasia and the Americas. It followed the success of European sea captains in permanently linking the two hemispheres. The ecological and demographic consequences of the Great Global Convergence were huge, especially the "Great Dying" of much of the indigenous population of the Americas. Europeans benefited from this disaster by peopling the Western Hemisphere with new immigrants, both free European settlers and African slaves. Europeans also gained access to important new sources of food and fiber. These included, among many others, maize (corn), tobacco, and the potato, which were American crops, and sugar and cotton, which came from Afroeurasia but thrived in American soil.

A third change was the emergence of a truly global economy. This was another consequence of the Great Global Convergence, which linked together all major regions, except Antarctica, in a single web of exchange. Silver was the great lubricator of global trade. In the 1550s, silver mined in the Americas became available to Spain, then to the rest of western Europe, as well as to China directly by way of Spanish galleon voyages across the Pacific Ocean. Silver financed Europe's increasing involvement in the economy

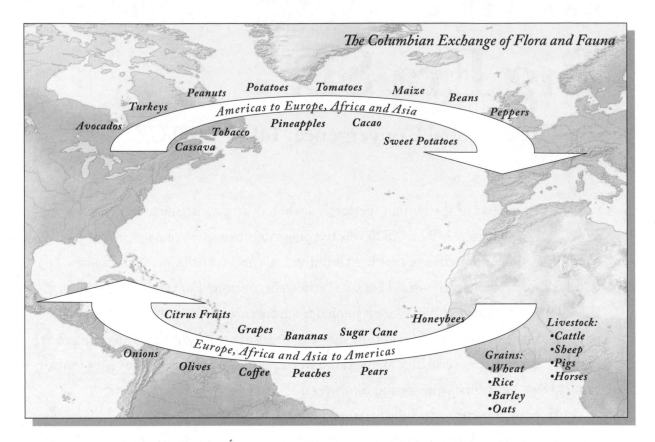

The Columbian Exchange of Flora and Fauna

of maritime Asia and subsequently provided the basis of the emergence of an Atlantic-centered world economy by 1800.

The remarkable rise of European political and military power relative to the rest of the world was the fourth major change. This was a consequence of 1) the spread to western Europe of technological and cultural innovations that originated elsewhere in Afroeurasia, and 2) western Europe's response to the challenges of warfare in the new age of gunpowder weapons. A complete transformation of the way people fought and paid for wars occurred first in Europe, then around the world. Historians have named this development the "military and fiscal revolution" because it involved unprecedented advances in military technology and in the methods governments used to raise public money for wars.

The fifth great change was the development in western Europe of the Scientific Revolution and the Enlightenment and the subsequent diffusion of their ideas to other parts of the world, as women and men grappled with them in a variety of ways. These intellectual and cultural developments helped to establish rational science as a standard for measuring and explaining the natural world and human behavior. They greatly enhanced human ability to manipulate nature. Because they challenged long-established religious and philosophical perspectives, these movements raised profound questions about ultimate meaning in nature and society and about the sources of knowledge. These questions continue to concern us today.

HUMANS AND THE ENVIRONMENT

Big Era Six was characterized by two contrasting major trends in human demography. On the one hand, it was a period of major population increase in Afroeurasia. The world's population increased from about 375 million in 1400 to 954 million in 1800. On the other hand, it saw a catastrophic collapse in the population of the Americas as a whole, which plummeted from at least 50 million in 1500 to perhaps 10 million by 1600.

Within these discordant trends, some important continuities may be seen. For example, as late as 1800, the end of Big Era Six, no more than about 2 percent of humans lived in cities, while 95 percent were farmers. The rest, about 3 percent, were foragers or pastoral nomads.

Consider differences in the population histories of these major world regions:

- China and India together had a population of around 140 million in 1400. At the end of Big Era Six they numbered 330 million and 180 million respectively.

- Europe's population went from about 52 million in 1400 to 146 million in 1800, with most of the increase coming in the eighteenth century.

- The population of Africa south of the Sahara was around 60 million in 1400 and may have reached 104 million by 1600. Because of the trans-Atlantic slave trade, numbers then declined, decreasing to about 92 million in 1800.

- The population of Latin America, which may have been 36 million in 1400, fell to 10 million by 1600. At this point, a gradual recovery set in, but by 1800 numbers had only recovered to about 19 million.

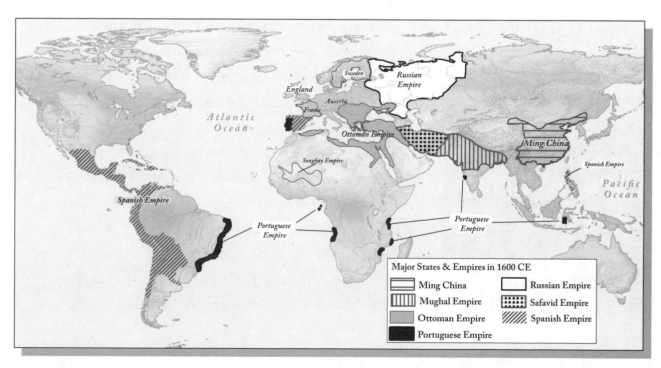

Regional Populations in Millions[10]

Area	1400 CE	1600 CE	1800 CE
China	70	110	330
India	74	145	180
Europe	52	89	146
Sub-Saharan Africa	60	104	92
Latin America	36	10	19

Why do you think population declined in Latin America between 1400 and 1600 CE and in Sub-Saharan Africa between 1600 and 1800 CE?

The Great Dying and Its Consequences

In the Western Hemisphere, the demographic collapse among Native Americans was catastrophic in places that had large populations on the eve of European contact. These places included the Caribbean islands, central Mexico, the Mayan highlands of southern Mexico and central America, and the Andes Mountains. The Great Dying involved multiple infectious diseases and ferocious pandemics that followed one after another for more than a century and a half. It began when new disease pathogens were inadvertently introduced to American Indian populations by early Spanish and Portuguese invaders. Owing to the long separation between the western and eastern hemispheres, the populations of the Americas had not evolved significant natural immunities to Afroeurasian infections, which included measles, smallpox, influenza, typhus, and tuberculosis. Therefore, they had no inherited defenses against them. In this perspective, the epidemic diseases can be seen as part of the Columbian Exchange of numerous organisms, including plants and animals.

The Great Dying caused massive social, economic, and cultural upheaval in numerous Amerindian societies. This was probably the major factor in the disintegration of the Aztec and Inca empires. The calamity also had a major impact on the development of the new Spanish empire in the Americas. The population loss meant that the Spanish faced severe shortages of labor and rapidly

> **The Great Dying... was probably the major factor in the disintegration of the Aztec and Inca empires.**

shrinking taxes. They therefore had to create an administrative system that gave priority to the mining industry and ensured the continued export of silver. Another consequence was the creation of social and legal institutions to force surviving Indian men and women to work for Europeans in mines and commercial agriculture.

The Great Dying, however, was just one aspect of the many ecological transformations that resulted from the Great Global Convergence. The arrival of Europeans in the Americas transformed the natural environment because the newcomers brought with them new organisms of all types, including many new food plants, several domestic animals (of which Native Americans had few), and numerous species of weeds. Because America's pre-existing biota was often unable to compete successfully with these invading species, much of the Western Hemisphere's environment came within several centuries to resemble the environment of northwestern Europe. In 1500, for example, wheat was unknown to peoples of North America. After European wheat-eaters introduced this crop to the North American temperate climate (which was not radically different from Europe's climate), it became a staple of the diet of most of the population. The same was true for the populations of the southern cone of South America.

The African Slave Trade

The Great Dying also set in motion another process: the forced migration of millions of African men and women across the Atlantic. This was because in order to keep the mines, plantations, and haciendas producing for the European market, European

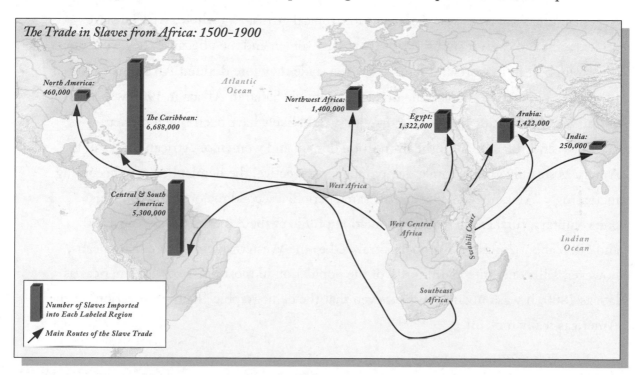

The Trade in Slaves from Africa: 1500–1900

North America: 460,000

The Caribbean: 6,688,000

Central & South America: 5,300,000

Atlantic Ocean

Northwest Africa: 1,400,000

Egypt: 1,322,000

Arabia: 1,422,000

India: 250,000

West Africa

West Central Africa

Swahili Coast

Indian Ocean

Southeast Africa

Number of Slaves Imported into Each Labeled Region

Main Routes of the Slave Trade

mine and estate owners had to find more labor. Because of the Great Dying, European entrepreneurs were frequently unable to find the local Indian labor they wanted, while free Europeans were unwilling to cross the Atlantic in large numbers to take up back-breaking jobs and expose themselves to tropical diseases. In order to continue making handsome profits from production and sale of sugar, silver, and other commodities, they brought in African slaves. From a sugar planter's point of view, African slaves—plentiful, cheap, and usually experienced at farming— were a practical solution.

This painting by François Auguste Biard entitled "The Slave Trade" depicts slaves on a ship making their way across the Atlantic to do forced labor in the Americas. How would you characterize the painter's interpretation of conditions on a slave ship and his attitude toward the Atlantic slave trade?

Between 1450 and 1810, perhaps 11 million enslaved Africans arrived in the Americas. European sea merchants contracted with African rulers and traders to sell them captured Africans who had been enslaved by fellow Africans in their homelands. Historians have estimated that 42 percent of these enslaved men and women were sent to the Caribbean, 38 percent to Brazil, and only 5 percent to North America. The slave trade was disastrous for tropical Africa as a whole. African slave traders aimed to capture and sell mainly young women and men because they were the age group best fit to work and reproduce. The trade therefore drained African societies of their most productive people. The population of Sub-Saharan Africa in 1900 was about 95 million. If the trade had not occurred, it would likely have been much higher.

Between 1500 and 1800 the proportion of men and women of African origin in the Americas steadily grew. From a demographic perspective, the hemisphere was becoming increasingly "Africanized." During the same period, a second major migration, this one voluntary, further altered the population profile of the Americas. Between 1500 and 1800 about 2 million Europeans traveled to the Western Hemisphere. Europeans, however, still constituted a minority of the population in most parts of the Americas as late as 1800. It was only in Big Era Seven that the demographic "Europeanization" of the Americas really took off.

Rampant Deforestation

Big Era Six witnessed a sharp increase in world deforestation, notably in Europe, the Americas, and Japan, an exploitation that also involved erosion, flooding, and climate change. The chief cause was the expansion of mining worldwide. This industry required vast quantities of wood, both fuel for smelters and timbers for mine shafts. This led to the deforestation of entire regions around the major mining sites. Silver and mercury mining in Japan and Latin America, notably Potosí and Huancavelica in the Peruvian Andes and Zacatecas in central Mexico, was especially destructive. Mining also significantly decreased forest cover in England, northern France, and central Europe.

The energy demands of the sugar industry in Brazil and the Caribbean, where biomass (wood) energy was needed to fire sugar boilers, produced extensive deforestation. Naval construction, which boomed during this period, was another major source of deforestation. The demands for ships' timbers, masts, and spars placed a severe strain upon the forests of the Baltic and New England, as well as those of the Indian Ocean rim, where vessels for the Asian trade were constructed.

Western Europe and Japan underwent profound energy crises in the seventeenth century due to deforestation. In Europe, the shortage of wood energy occasioned a search for alternative sources, provoking the shift to fossil fuels, initially coal. In Japan, by contrast, the wood crisis led to an ambitious reforestation project. This said, we must note that most of the switch from biomass to fossil fuels occurred in the subsequent Big Era.

HUMANS AND OTHER HUMANS

The most important change affecting the relationships of humans with one another in this period was the transformation in social organization. Important developments included larger and more efficient bureaucratic states, as well as more complex systems of communication and economic exchange. Changes in the scale and complexity of human interactions greatly favored elites, that is people with wealth and power, because they were able to control and manage the new forms of organization and technology. Ordinary people, however, could also use new types of communication to promote social, religious, or political reform.

Far-reaching changes in maritime ship-building and navigation greatly speeded global

> **Changes in the scale and complexity of human interactions greatly favored elites, that is people with wealth and power.**

exchange in Big Era Six. New maritime technology, plus the European innovation of mounting cannons on shipboard, supported the rise of the Spanish, Portuguese, Dutch, British, and French maritime empires. These empires were larger and more diverse than earlier ones. New firearms technology also contributed to the expansion of Afroeurasian land empires that were better organized for controlling their subjects and collecting taxes than were earlier empires. These states included the Turkish Ottoman, Safavid Persian, Mughal Indian, Chinese, and Russian empires, plus others in Inner Eurasia, West Africa, and Southeast Asia.

By contrast, the Aztec and Inca empires in the Americas, though impressive in size, resembled earlier agrarian states of Afroeurasia, not the new "gunpowder empires." Their lack of firearms, iron tools and weapons, long-distance transport ships, horse cavalry, and other technologies possessed by Europeans contributed to their sudden collapse. Even so, had there been no gunpowder the Spanish conquests in the Americas would almost certainly have taken longer.

A Shift in the Economic Center of Gravity

Asia was the center of global economic activity at the beginning of Big Era Six. Then a shift westward toward Europe began to occur, though not until the later eighteenth century. How did this come about, and what were the main consequences? The linking of Afroeurasia with the Americas was the most important factor. The sudden arrival in the sixteenth century of vast quantities of silver in world markets led to a rapid increase in commercial exchanges of all kinds. This was as true for Asia, where the economies of both China and India were based on silver coinage, as it was for Europe. Likewise, America was supplying increasing amounts of precious metals to the world market. In the long run, it seems clear that Europeans benefited the most from this development. But this was not apparent in the sixteenth century.

> Asia was the center of global economic activity at the beginning of Big Era Six.

In the early part of Big Era Six, European participation in the trade of Asia was seriously limited. Europeans did not produce any commodities or finished goods that Asians wanted to buy. American silver, which Native Americans and African slaves extracted from the earth, provided a solution for European entrepreneurs. They could purchase Asian commodities (pepper, spices, coffee, tea, porcelain, carpets, silk, and cotton cloth) with American silver and, to some extent, gold. Once Europeans with precious metals to sell entered the trade of Asia, they also profited as specialists in moving goods from one part of Asia or Africa to another—Chinese porcelain to India, for example, or Indian textiles to West Africa. The trade boom in maritime Asia soared to new heights between the sixteenth and eighteenth centuries. But this boom greatly benefited European states and merchants as well as Asian ones.

> **...In parts of tropical Africa, the slave trade removed so many young males from society that women came significantly to outnumber men.**

Changing conditions of production, consumption, and labor around the world greatly affected the lives of ordinary women and men. These transformations took place in work habits, incomes, diet, family structure, and in some places even the ratio of women to men. For example, in parts of tropical Africa, the slave trade removed so many young males from society that women came significantly to outnumber men. By contrast, in the densest plantation societies in the Caribbean and Brazil, enslaved men of African descent greatly outnumbered enslaved women.

Sugar itself had a transforming effect on the Atlantic world in Big Era Six. The sugar boom brought riches to some Europeans and Africans but a death sentence to many others. The swelling consumption of sugar, coffee, tea, and cacao transformed the diets and daily habits of ordinary Europeans and linked them by invisible economic threads to enslaved Caribbean and Brazilian workers. The silver mines and sugar plantations did much to create a new international division of labor in which Africans, Native Americans, and Asians increasingly supplied labor and raw materials, while Europeans made finished goods using complex technologies.

Revolution in Military Power and Finance

A primary reason for the rise of European power was the military and fiscal revolution. In the military sphere, Europeans adopted gunpowder weaponry, which had originally been pioneered in China. This soon led to advances in strategy, tactics, fort-building, and discipline. Warfare became the business of professional soldiers and sailors. Europeans fought many wars during this Big Era. These conflicts included the

The emperor of Russia ordered the casting of the "Tsar Cannon" in 1586. Made of bronze, its tube weighs 40 tons. It was intended for defense of the Kremlin in Moscow, but it was never fired.

Wars of Religion, the Puritan Revolution in England, the Seven Years' War, the American War of Independence, and the French Revolution. Military innovations, however, did not serve all European states equally because some states augmented their power at the expense of others. By 1800, Britain had virtually eliminated France, its principal rival for global domination, from North America, the Caribbean, and South Asia.

The military revolution was also fiscal because it required deep changes in state bureaucracy, taxation, and accounting to pay for increasingly expensive wars. In this race for revenue only the fiscally fit survived. The power of states unable to finance costly artillery and other weapons was gradually reduced by their more successful rivals. Britain's greater ability to finance warfare largely explains its victories over France. For example, French military and financial support for the American Revolution led to that kingdom's bankruptcy and thus contributed to the French Revolution, to be discussed in Big Era Seven. In Asia, imperial states like the Ottomans, Mughals, and Ming Chinese adopted gunpowder weapons and expanded their territories. They did not, however, accept the full package of military and fiscal reforms that Europeans did. By the later eighteenth century, the balance of military power in the world was shifting to the European side.

Before the nineteenth century, European states did not have a significant military advantage over Asian or African rivals. For example, at the start of the era, the Austrian Hapsburg empire (the largest in Europe) could not defeat the Ottoman Turkish empire, its principal rival. The Portuguese, Dutch, and English traded for slaves in West Africa but seized little territory because regional African states, which were increasingly armed with guns, had sufficient power to defend themselves. The tropical disease environment in West Africa was also deadly to Europeans. It was not until the nineteenth century that Europeans began to have

Before the nineteenth century, European states did not have a significant military advantage over Asian or African rivals.

adequate military and medical technology to readily defeat Asian or African armies. At the start of Big Era Seven, for example, both Austrian and Russian forces deploying massed field artillery and other lethal weapons were able to defeat the Ottomans more and more often.

HUMANS AND IDEAS

In Big Era Six, Europe emerged as a center of technological and scientific advance, a hotbed of ideas and inventions that contributed greatly to the building of denser networks of human interaction. It is important to note, however, that Europe enjoyed this role only because its thinkers and experimenters were able to build on the legacy of scientific and technological exchanges that had been part of Afroeurasian history for several millennia. As we have suggested in the discussion for the previous Big Eras, between the eighth and fourteenth centuries, a new synthesis of Arab, Persian, Mesopotamian, Greek, and Indian knowledge about nature, society, and the cosmos gradually appeared. Beginning in the twelfth century, Europeans gradually adopted this synthesis of learning and increasingly contributed to it.

A self-portrait of Sofonisba Anguissola. This Italian Renaissance artist was painter to the royal court of the Emperor Philip II of Spain. Among the artists of the European Renaissance that we know about, why do you think men far outnumber women?

Cultural Developments in Europe

Europe's transformation was also the product of internal cultural trends. Following its recovery from the devastating plagues, climatic deterioration, and warfare of the fourteenth century, Europe underwent a multi-dimensional revival. Its most visible cultural sign was the Renaissance, a flowering of art, literature, philosophy, and science centered in (and paid for by) royal courts and wealthy men and women in Italy and, a bit later, in northwestern Europe. The Renaissance was a cultural expression of Europe's new prosperity, and it was fed by the new knowledge that poured into the region in the wake of European explorations and conquests across the oceans. In world terms, however, the Renaissance was not a major cultural turning point. Rather, it raised the level of sophistication and refinement of European elite culture to that of urban societies in the rest of Afroeurasia. A more decisive transformation was the Scientific Revolution that came in the seventeenth century.

One critical innovation was the printing press and the use of movable type, which Johannes Gutenberg (1394–1468) pioneered in Europe in the late fifteenth century.

A replica of the Gutenberg press

Printing using movable type had existed for many centuries in East Asia. Korean artisans invented the use of metal movable type, as opposed to wood or ceramic type, about the same time that Gutenberg was experimenting with movable type. This technology, however, caught on especially fast in western Europe. Printing stimulated literacy among middle- and upper-class Europeans, a growing market for ideas, including new conceptions of nature, the cosmos, and human society.

The spread of Protestantism was a major development linked to printing. The Protestant Reformation was a movement of religious protest and reform that burst on the European scene in the early sixteenth century. Martin Luther (1483–1546), a German Christian monk, challenged the Roman Catholic Church to make numerous reforms in doctrine and leadership. The result was a long and bitter struggle for religious and political power that divided western Europeans for well over a century. At the same time, the Catholic Church continued to gain followers, and a variety of Protestant churches sprang up, the forerunners of modern denominations such as the Lutherans, Presbyterians, Methodists, Episcopalians, and Baptists.

The Global Religious Scene

European merchants, soldiers, and missionaries also took Christianity, both Catholic and Protestant, around the world, leading to its rapid spread, especially in the Americas. Islam, an alternative vision of belief in one God, also continued to expand across

Afroeurasia, carried along the overland routes and long-distance sea lanes. While Christianity was sinking deep roots in the Americas, Islam gained millions of new adherents in West Africa, East Africa, southeastern Europe, Inner Eurasia, India, and Southeast Asia. Buddhism continued to grow in China, Japan, and Southeast Asia.

The Djinguareben mosque in Timbuktu, Mali, West Africa

However, the major organized faiths—Christianity, Islam, Buddhism, Daoism, Hinduism, and Judaism—had nothing like a monopoly on religious belief and practice in the world. Many believers in the major religions knew very little about the formal doctrines of their own faiths. They lived, rather, in a world dominated by beliefs in magic and spirits. Local, polytheistic religions declined on a world scale but continued to thrive in more remote places. Also, faiths involving syncretism, which means the meshing of beliefs and rituals of different traditions, became more common as the web of human interactions around the world tightened.

The Scientific Revolution

In Europe, the fragmenting of religious doctrine that accompanied the Protestant Reformation, the sudden linkup with the Americas, and the continuing flow of

European merchants, soldiers, and missionaries also took Christianity, both Catholic and Protestant, around the world, leading to its rapid spread, especially in the Americas.

knowledge from distant parts of Afroeurasia produced multiple shocks to the Christian worldview. Such newness and change provoked a searching examination of the place of humans in the cosmos and nature. In the absence of any single controlling religious authority to stop them, scholars like Copernicus, Galileo, Descartes, Pascal, and Newton put forward philosophical and scientific ideas that challenged older ways of thinking.

Most important, they argued that the universe operates according to natural laws, which human reason and careful observation may discover and explain. The resulting

Scientific Revolution was in many ways the logical outcome of Afroeurasia's total legacy of scientific and philosophical creativity. It was also, however, a dramatic break with the long world trend to rely mainly on priests, spiritual sages, and other religious authorities to explain all things. In the eighteenth century, the Enlightenment, a great debate over the relative merits of science and faith as the proper measure of reality, gathered steam in Europe and began to penetrate other parts of the world.

CHAPTER 6 STUDY QUESTIONS

1. In terms of population, urbanization, technology, and economy, Europe was not as important a region as some others in the world before 1500. What factors do you think contributed to Europe's growing importance in these respects after 1500?

2. Define the Columbian Exchange and explain why far more plant species, animals species, disease microorganisms, and people flowed from Afroeurasia to the Americas than in the opposite direction in the sixteenth and seventeenth centuries.

3. What are some of the important ways in which the discovery of large quantities of silver in the Americas in the sixteenth century affected the world economy and large regions such as China, India, or Europe?

4. Would you agree or disagree that economic inequality grew in the world during Big Era Six? Offer evidence to support your position.

5. "The Scientific Revolution was a logical outcome of Afroeurasia's total legacy of scientific and philosophical creativity." Do you agree with this statement? Why or why not?

Big Era Seven

Industrialization and Its Consequences, 1750–1914 CE

The period from 1750 to 1914 was a pivotal moment in human history. Historians have named it the era of the "modern revolution." Over the course of Big Era Seven, change in human society became "autocatalytic." Scientists use this term to describe a chemical process, but it is also a useful historical concept. A catalyst is a person or thing that precipitates a change. Autocatalysis occurs when one kind of change precipitates by itself the need for other kinds of changes. Since about 1750, a steadily pyramiding sequence of changes has transformed human life. Moreover, the dynamic interactions among changes in many different areas—political, economic, technological, cultural, environmental—have, by the very process of interaction, generated the need for even more changes. Once autocatalytic processes got going, they tended to speed up. Overall, global changes have become self-perpetuating and ever-accelerating.

The modern revolution involved numerous interacting developments. Six interrelated factors were particularly important:

First, a revolutionary transformation occurred in human use of energy. Until the nineteenth century, the energy basis of human society had been biomass energy, mainly the burning of wood to produce heat, plus human and animal muscle power. With Big Era Seven, the world entered the age of coal and steam power. The fossil fuel era had begun, and this is the era we still live in today. By the early nineteenth century, the harnessing of steam power enabled humans to vastly multiply the energy generated from burning coal, thereby greatly expanding the amount of energy available to humans per capita, that is, to each individual. By 1914, petroleum, a second major fossil fuel, began to be extensively used as well. Natural gas is the third important fossil fuel.

Second, unprecedented global population growth accompanied the fossil fuel revolution. In Big Era Seven the world's population more than doubled, definitively piercing the previous limits on growth. In 1800, the global population stood at around 900 million, by itself a huge leap from the start of the previous era. By 1914, it stood at around 1.75 billion people. The great increase in human numbers is a sign that major changes were at work.

Third, an industrial transformation got under way. In the Industrial Revolution, humans—western Europeans at first—learned to exploit coal and steam energy to mass produce goods with machines and to sell them worldwide. The Industrial Revolution began with production of textiles and eventually spread to other areas of manufacturing, as well as to farming and food processing. In the later nineteenth century, industrialization occurred on a large scale in metallurgical, chemical, and electrical industries. Once begun, it could not be stopped. The Industrial Revolution greatly altered the distribution of wealth and poverty around the world and also engendered new attitudes towards nature and society.

Fourth, a revolution took place in communications and transport. Unprecedented numbers of people in this era took advantage of steamships and railroads to migrate long distances within continental spaces as well as across oceans. European migrants were especially attracted to areas such as North America and the southern cone of South America where the climate was reasonably familiar. Asian migrants, especially South Asians and Chinese, settled in many parts of the tropical world as well as in the Americas.

> **The Industrial Revolution greatly altered the distribution of wealth and poverty around the world and engendered new attitudes towards nature and society.**

Fifth, the modern revolution was partly a democratic revolution. Popular revolutionary movements of the late eighteenth and early nineteenth centuries dramatically reshaped ideas about government and political power. While these movements were initially centered on countries around the rim of the Atlantic, their ideas proved contagious, provoking movements for the abolition of slavery, representative government, constitutions, universal suffrage, workers' rights, gender equality, and national self-determination, first in Europe and the Americas, later all across Afroeurasia.

Finally, the era witnessed the rise of new colonial empires. Using new technologies of warfare and political control that came out of the Industrial Revolution, the empires of several European states greatly increased in size during this era. The United States, Russia, and Japan also drew on these new capabilities to expand their own empires. All of the imperial states adopted elaborate racial justifications for dominance over other peoples.

HUMANS AND THE ENVIRONMENT

The fossil fuel revolution was a fundamental breakthrough in human history. It was as significant for our species as the transition to agriculture. Coal contains much higher levels of energy per given weight than equivalent amounts of renewable biomass (wood). Exploiting coal on a large scale, humans were able to burst through the ceiling on economic growth that had been in place since the modern human species appeared around 200,000 BP.

At the start of Big Era Seven, world coal output per year was less than 10 million metric tons. Then things began to change, thanks mainly to steam-powered pump engines, which allowed coal miners to drain the water that tended to accumulate in mine shafts and tunnels. By 1860, the world produced about 130 million tons of coal. In 1900, production rose to an astonishing 1 billion tons, and coal provided 90 percent of total world energy consumption.

Many More People

A second major source of environmental change was population growth. In 1700, world population, according to one estimate, was about 603.4 million. By 1913, it had nearly tripled to about 1.79 billion. The environmental impact of this dramatic population increase, combined with the surges in economic growth and energy consumption, was colossal. Let us consider some major factors.

A coal mine in the Rhondda Valley, a major mining region in Wales in the 19th century. What 18th-century invention made it possible for coal miners to extend shafts and tunnels deep underground?

At first, the population increase was disproportionately concentrated in western Europe, where numbers increased from 81.4 million in 1700 to 261 million in 1913, despite the emigration of millions of Europeans to overseas states and colonies. Later in the era, the populations of Asia and Latin America also increased dramatically. For example, Asia's population (excluding Japan) grew from 374.8 million in 1700 to 925.9 million in 1913, an increase of nearly two and a half times its population.

In some isolated regions, notably Siberia, Australia, many Pacific islands, and some areas of tropical rainforest, indigenous populations declined. This was mainly because outsiders introduced infectious diseases to which the inhabitants had weak immunities. Epidemics were sometimes locally catastrophic, comparable to the Great Dying in the Americas relative to population size. In the late eighteenth century, for example, a pestilence on the Siberian peninsula of Kamchatka carried off as many as 75 percent of the local inhabitants. When European settlers started arriving in New Zealand in 1840, the indigenous Maori population may have numbered 100,000 or more. By 1858, it declined to 56,000, owing mainly to diseases that Europeans brought with them.

Rapid urbanization accompanied world population growth. In 1800, only nine cities in the world had a population of 1 million or more. By 1900, twenty-seven cities had more than 1 million people. The proportion of the world's people who lived in cities, rather than in rural areas, increased from 2 percent in 1800 to 10 percent in 1900.

World Population Trends in Millions (1700–1913)

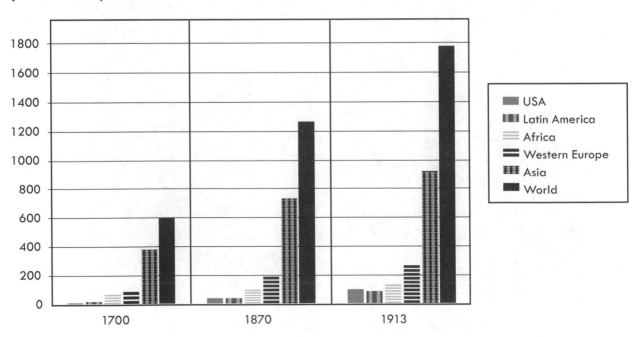

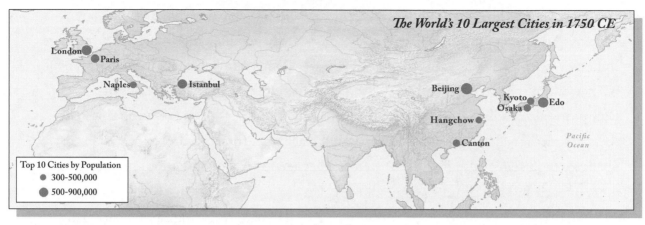

How would you account for the changes in the locations of the top ten cities in the world between 1750 and 1900?

Mass Migrations

Steamships and railroads made major migrations of peoples possible in Big Era Seven. More than 50 million people emigrated from Europe (including Russia) during the era, two-thirds of them permanently. Most of them were looking for work, opportunity, and the prospect of higher living standards than they had enjoyed in their native lands. Their destinations were mainly the world's temperate zones: Canada, the United States, Algeria, and Siberia in the Northern Hemisphere; Chile, Argentina, Uruguay, South Africa, Australia, and New Zealand in the Southern Hemisphere.

Indigenous peoples resisted these newcomers, but in many places they were eventually demographically swamped by them. For example, the population of the territory that now constitutes the United States

The proportion of the world's people who lived in cities, rather than in rural areas, increased from 2 percent in 1800 to 10 percent in 1900.

may have been as high as 10 million in 1500, and those people were all American Indians. According to the 2000 census, by contrast, the population classified as American Indian or Native Alaskan numbered just over 2 million, a number representing only about 0.7 percent of the total population of 281.4 million. These overseas migrations of Europeans also had a significant environmental impact. This is because Europeans and their descendants possessed both sophisticated machine technology and expectations of relatively high standards of living. Therefore, they tended to exploit natural resources more intensively than did the peoples they replaced.

This 1870 newspaper clipping depicts immigrants "leaving old England for America."

Another pattern of migration continued from the previous Big Era. Between 1750 and 1870, about 1.7 million Africans were moved involuntarily to the Americas, most of them destined to work on sugar and coffee plantations in Brazil or the Caribbean. After 1800, however, the proportion of people of African descent living in the Americas declined relative to the number of people of European ancestry. This happened because so many more Europeans migrated to the Americas in the nineteenth century than did before 1800. Also, the average life span of African slaves was significantly lower than that of European immigrants to the Americas.

A third pattern was the migration of Asian laborers. Between 1830 and 1913, some 30 to 40 million Indians and about 15 million Chinese left their countries to seek work in mines and on plantations in European colonies and Latin American countries, as well as in Southeast Asia, the Pacific islands, and South Africa. In the earlier decades of the century, many Asians migrated under contracts of indenture, which offered them free or cheap transport in return for a specified number of years of employment. Many indentured migrants were treated unfairly and left worse off than they had been at home. Many Asians migrated to the U.S., Canada, and Australia to build railroads. Many became permanent settlers, though others eventually returned home.

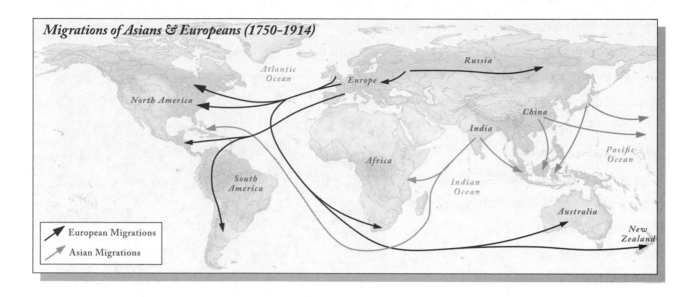

Migrations of Asians & Europeans (1750-1914)

By one estimate, more than 100 million people worldwide were involved in long-distance migrations during Big Era Seven. Finally, we must also mention the millions more who migrated within the lands of their birth to seek work and opportunity in cities or other regions of economic growth. Internal migrations were an important aspect of change in India, China, Russia, the Ottoman empire, Africa, and Latin America.

Environmental Impact of Industrialization And Migration

The Industrial Revolution transformed the ability of humans to reshape the world's environment. Deforestation increased on a global scale. So too did water pollution from chemical and agricultural discharges into lakes and streams, and atmospheric pollution from the burning of huge amounts of coal. The advent of railroads and steamships also hastened the diffusion of plants and animals to new parts of the world. This was an extension of the Columbian Exchange of biota that occurred in the previous Big Era. The spread of new plants, such as maize, wheat, and cassava into areas where they had previously been unknown, underwrote large population increases. But environmentally adverse consequences also occurred. For example, in 1859 a farmer in Australia introduced a few rabbits for hunting. Within a few years rabbits were hopping across the continent by the millions, ravaging crops as they went. By 1950, Australia's rabbit population numbered 500 million and continued to wreak havoc on agriculture.

Despite the global economic advances of Big Era Seven, several major famines occurred. In fact, famines intensified as a result of increased global economic integration, which sometimes devastated peasant societies and sharpened social inequalities. In 1846–49, for example, a series of regional blights ruined potato harvests in Ireland and Eastern Europe. The resulting food deficit provoked many deaths and mass migrations. Even more distressing were the famines of 1876–1902, which historians have linked to climatic conditions produced by the El Niño Southern Oscillation (ENSO), a cyclical warming of sea surface temperatures combined with changes in sea level pressure in the southern Pacific basin. Although grain was available to feed the hungry, colonial economic policies justified its continued export to industrial countries for profit. Millions died in parts of Africa, Asia, and Latin America, and countless millions more were reduced to poverty. Some historians believe that the late nineteenth century famines, coming when they did, were instrumental in producing the gap in living standards that subsequently divided the developed from the underdeveloped world.

Victims of famine in India

> The term "liberal" refers basically to an attitude that favors individual rights, free markets, representative government, and progress. In Big Era Seven, liberalism took the form of a complex "package" of ideas and plans of action.

HUMANS AND OTHER HUMANS

In Big Era Seven, autocatalytic change prevailed as ecological, economic, political, and technological developments fed upon one another and merged into a single global process, the modern revolution. This revolution was global in scope and fundamentally irreversible.

As peoples around the world, especially elite groups with power and wealth, attempted to understand and influence the multitude of new developments that constituted the modern revolution, the doctrines of liberalism came to the fore, first of all in Europe and the United States. The term "liberal" refers basically to an attitude that favors individual rights, free markets, representative government, and progress. In Big Era Seven, liberalism took the form of a complex "package" of ideas and plans of action.

In the economic sphere, liberalism called for such reforms as establishment of the rule of law in societies, the sanctity of private property, and the improvement of communications, including railroads, steamship lines, telegraphs, and modern port facilities. Liberal economic reformers believed the market to be the ultimate governor of human relations, and they insisted that both property and labor be released from the outmoded restrictions of medieval times.

In politics, liberal reformers called for republican (that is, representative) government characterized by democratic participation, constitutions, and legislatures. They also demanded the separation of church and state and an end to policies that allowed churches to be exempt from taxes and to control primary education.

Economic Trends

In the first phase of the Industrial Revolution (1750–1840), entrepreneurs and workers harnessed coal and steam power to drive industrial machinery and vastly increase production. This development occurred first in England. Railroads drastically lowered the cost of land transportation, while greatly increasing the volume of goods and persons transported, as well as the speed at which they were moved. Consequently, railroads were especially important in large countries such as the United States and Russia. Railroad construction also propelled coal and steel industries and facilitated the expansion of markets. After 1840, and especially after 1860, steam-generated electricity powered industrial machinery.

Also, the modern world economy became increasingly organized on the basis of an international division of labor. This meant that colonial possessions and other rural regions of the world produced mainly raw materials for export. In return, they imported finished goods from the metropolitan country (the one that controlled the colony) and from industrializing regions generally.

Around 1800, for example, sugar was the world's most important commercial crop. It was produced by slave labor and made great profits for sugar merchants, plantation owners, and financiers, mainly in Europe. By the 1830s, sugar was supplanted by cotton as the leading market crop. This happened mainly owing to the industrial mechanization of cotton textile production. In the Americas, cotton continued to be produced by slaves; in countries like Egypt and India, peasants grew it for small returns. Since British soil could not produce cotton, factories had to import all of it from India, Egypt, and the southern United States. British manufacturers inundated the world market with cotton products. For British manufacturers, this was good liberal practice because the market was allowed to determine whether Indians bought local or European cottons. The market, however, drove down prices of handloom cotton in India and destroyed the livelihood of local spinners and weavers there. Many of those artisans ended up growing raw cotton and selling it to merchants for export to European factories.

The World's Six Longest Railroad Networks (1845–1940)

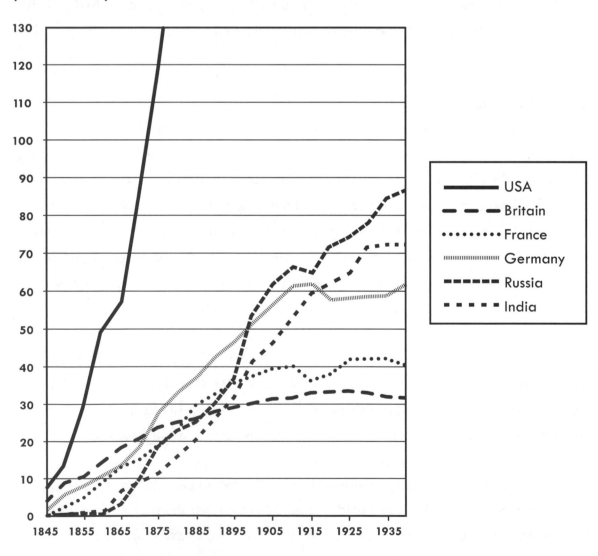

What factors might help explain the relative growth rate and length of these six networks?

The British iron steamship *HMS Nemesis* destroying Chinese war junks in the Opium War, 1841

When necessary, however, European powers were willing to gain economic advantages using strategies that contradicted the free market. In the previous big era, Asians had been mostly unwilling to import European goods because they did not want or need them. This had been a key economic weakness for European manufacturers and merchants. As a result of the Opium War (1839–1842), however, Britain used naval force to compel the Chinese government to open its market to opium grown in India, then a British colony. This traffic enabled Britain to balance its trade with China for the first time in history. Following the war, the British government imposed a series of treaties on China that gave Britain favored and unequal trading privileges. British merchants regarded this course of events as a case of practical liberal reform, but it led to a large flow of silver out of China to pay for opium, which weakened the already strained Chinese economy. It also led to debilitating opium addictions for millions of Chinese.

In the second half of the era, European and American governments followed suit, establishing, by armed intervention, privileged enclaves in Southeast Asia and China. In 1854, Japan also had to sign an unequal treaty with the United States and then with major European powers. These unequal treaties were the norm not only for European trade with Asia but also with Latin America and the Middle East. States wishing to trade with Britain had to set low tariffs on British imports and adopt legal and other measures favorable to British interests. In the course of the nineteenth century, other European countries, as well as the United States, imposed similarly unfavorable commercial treaties on many countries.

Following the discovery of gold in California in 1849 and later discoveries in Australia, Alaska, and South Africa, a new cycle of global economic growth set in. The increased availability of this precious metal led in 1878 to the establishment of the gold standard, which fixed the value of all currencies in terms of gold. For the first time, there was a single global financial market, which liberals regarded as a progressive reform. For others, the gold standard set up terms of trade that led to the impoverishment of their countries.

Between 1880 and 1914, the world economy underwent a second major wave of expansion. Global growth increased threefold, world trade fourfold, and international investment eightfold. The modern communications revolution, including the building of railroads in Africa, Asia, and Latin America, the global expansion of steamship travel, the laying of the trans-oceanic telegraph cables, and the invention of the telephone, greatly enhanced the movement of peoples, goods, and capital worldwide. The mechanization of agriculture in both Europe and temperate regions where Europeans settled made it possible to produce, process, and transport food more cheaply and efficiently. The steel and chemical industries emerged as a new focus of production and profit just when innovations in the textile industry were slowing down.

> The dark side of wealth accumulation was that increased integration of the world market made economies more vulnerable to financial crashes that could wipe out vast sums in a moment.

The era also saw major economic consolidation. In accord with liberal principles that valued accumulation of private capital and the sanctity of property, new cartels and trusts were formed whose wealth dwarfed any business organizations previously known in history. Two examples were U.S. Steel and Unilever Brothers. The dark side of wealth accumulation was that increased integration of the world market made economies more vulnerable to financial crashes that could wipe out vast sums in a moment.

Political Trends

Big Era Seven began with the rise of Britain as the leading global power, overshadowing France and all other countries. The Seven Years' War and the American

Revolution bankrupted France and stripped it of nearly all its possessions in Canada and India. But despite Britain's great power, it still had to accommodate itself to the consequences of the revolutions that occurred in the Thirteen Colonies of North America, France, Haiti, and the Latin American colonies of Spain between 1774 and 1830.

The revolution in the British Thirteen Colonies of North America was the first of the Atlantic revolutions. The others were the French Revolution (1789–99), the Haitian Revolution (1791-1804), and several revolutionary movements in Latin America (1810–28). In both the United States and Latin America, revolutions involved the founding of republics dominated by affluent middle classes. Voting was at first confined to property-holding adult males, and slavery was left largely undisturbed. Nevertheless, the visible contrast between the huge profits made by plantation owners and the misery of laboring slaves provided an engine for political change. The anti-slavery movement was an important part of liberal reform in the Americas in the first half of Big Era Seven. The success of the revolution on the French-ruled island of Saint Domingue in 1804 ended slavery there and produced the Republic of Haiti, the world's first state governed by descendants of enslaved African immigrants.

Prior to 1789, kingship provided the dominant political model ever since the origins of civilization. Following the French Revolution, individuals would no longer be subjects of monarchs who ruled by "divine right." Instead, they became citizens possessing specific rights and duties embodied in a system of laws, to be enacted by legislatures composed of the people's elected representatives. This represented a major change in human political organization. Between 1789 and 1914, many monarchies were replaced by republics throughout the world, though the degree of democratic participation in these republics varied widely. Or, as in the British example, monarchs were made subordinate to parliaments and other democratic institutions.

> In both the United States and Latin America, revolutions involved the founding of republics dominated by affluent middle classes.

Henceforth, kings had to respond to pressure from liberal-minded elites to incorporate democratic political features, such as constitutions and elected assemblies.

Another major political transformation was the abolition of slavery. As a result of decades of anti-slavery protests, the British and American governments abolished the slave trade in 1807 and slavery as a legal institution in Britain's colonies in 1833.

The defeat of slavery, however, was incomplete. For one thing, other European states, like Spain, France, and Portugal, failed to follow the British example immediately. Also, slavery continued in the United States until its abolition in 1865, after a bitter and protracted civil war. Brazil and Cuba did not abolish slavery until the late 1880s. Serfdom, a different form of unfree labor, was abolished in Russia in 1861. That being said, it is important to recognize that slavery was replaced by other forms of coerced labor, such as indentured labor.

Overall, liberal political and economic ideas provoked great opposition and struggle. While some elites, notably merchants, manufacturers, government bureaucrats, educators, and some church leaders endeavored to implement the liberal reform package of rights and representation, other groups steadfastly resisted these reforms. Opposition came especially from commercial planters, established landowners, military officers, and some religious authorities. In societies as diverse as Mexico, Brazil, Egypt, Turkey, China, and Japan, attempts to implement a liberal reform package divided elites and caused prolonged social struggles. From a global perspective, the civil war, abolition, and reconstruction in the United States fit into this pattern of conflict between liberal and anti-liberal forces.

> **Another major political transformation was the abolition of slavery.**

Colonial Encounters

The modern revolution deepened the extremes of wealth and poverty in the world, and the expansion of European colonial empires greatly widened this gap. Colonial rule assumed many forms and produced contradictory results. In South Asia, Britain spent much of the era incorporating numerous pre-existing territories and kingdoms into a unified Indian colonial empire. In Africa and mainland Southeast Asia, the chronology was different. Before the 1870s, European territorial expansion in Africa was largely confined to Algeria and South Africa. In Southeast Asia, the Dutch ruled part, though not nearly all, of Indonesia. From the 1870s to 1914, however, most of Africa, with the exceptions of Ethiopia and Liberia, came under some form of European colonial rule. In Southeast Asia, Britain expanded in Burma; France in Vietnam, Cambodia, and Laos; and the Netherlands in more remote parts of Indonesia. European expectations of new wealth and markets impelled much of this expansion.

In all these places local populations resisted European takeover, sometimes mustering large military forces, sometimes fighting in guerrilla bands, sometimes striving for religious or political reforms that might keep invaders at bay. However, European forces equipped with up-to-date weapons, including portable artillery and the Maxim gun, an early form of machine gun, put down almost all organized resistance. Once they set up their colonial governments, they proceeded with systematic extraction of raw materials from their colonies, including rubber, cacao, peanuts, tropical oils, and minerals. In 1800, Europeans controlled some 35 percent of the earth's land area. By 1914, they dominated about 88 percent.

> The modern revolution deepened the extremes of wealth and poverty in the world, and the expansion of European colonial empires greatly widened this gap.

HUMANS AND IDEAS

In Big Era Seven the ideas of the Scientific Revolution and the Enlightenment sank deep roots in Europe and spread widely to other parts of the world, especially within elite culture and city-dwelling middle classes. On the other hand, peasants and workers who could not read and write tended to be unacquainted with these ideas, at least until later periods.

The Rise of Secularism

For liberals, human progress was obviously desirable and inevitable, and science challenged earlier understandings of nature and the universe. Many educated people in Europe saw experimental science as a rival of religion as a system of thought. Opponents of reform, however, deplored the dizzying change and the weakening of religious and moral traditions. In fact, the modern revolution set off a major cultural struggle between advocates of science and defenders of traditional religions. Scientific explanations of the universe assumed that things happened without intention or purpose and that the universe was inanimate, rather than a manifestation of supernatural power. Scientific perspectives on the earth's geology challenged the biblical story of the Great

Flood, while Charles Darwin's book *The Origin of Species* (1859) provided a new perspective on the place of humans in the scheme of nature. Gradually a secular (that is, "worldly" or non-sacred) culture emerged that accepted the premises of modern science and challenged the cultural dominance of religious organizations and doctrines.

This "secularization" was an important part of the modern revolution, first spreading through Europe, then throughout the rest of the world. Advocates and opponents of secularization struggled mightily over many issues, including the role of religious institutions in education, the rights and privileges of religious denominations, and the place of women in public life. Liberal-minded secularists believed that science and technology would inevitably banish superstition and

In the Battle of Adowa in Ethiopia in 1896, a well-armed Ethiopian force under the command of King Menelik II defeated an Italian army. Ethiopia was the only African country to defend itself successfully against European invasion in the late 19th century. Which figure in this painting might be King Menelik II?

backwardness. Christian, Muslim, Jewish, and other believers argued that scientific explanations dismissed God, undermined moral standards, and left humans without spiritual guidance or direction.

> Christian, Muslim, Jewish, and other believers argued that scientific explanations dismissed God, undermined moral standards, and left humans without spiritual guidance or direction.

Most leaders of secular culture also believed that progress was a uniquely European idea generously made available to the world. Many even used Darwin's theory of evolution to demonstrate the racial and moral superiority of Europeans over other peoples on the grounds that Europeans were making more material progress than others and were therefore the "fittest" members of the human species.

Nineteenth-Century Racism

This distortion of Darwinism became a justification for racism and colonial rule. Suspicion and disdain among social and cultural groups, who regarded one another as strange and inferior, had been common in world history for millennia. What emerged in Europe, however, was a supposedly scientific racism that cloaked theories of European racial superiority in the vocabulary and methods of modern biology and anthropology. This "pseudo-science" provided a moral justification for both colonial conquest and the systems of inequality that governed colonial societies. Popular race theories had in fact no sound basis in science, but this seemed of no consequence to those who wished to justify imperial rule and economic exploitation of colonial labor and resources.

Charles Darwin, 1809–1882. He authored *The Origin of Species*.

Thriving Religions

The advance of secular culture challenged the world's religions, but, even so, most of the major faiths grew at a faster pace than ever. The printing of religious scriptures and other theological and spiritual writings, as well as their global dissemination, tended to make beliefs and practices within the leading religions more uniform. Propelled by the new communications technologies, Christian missionaries of various denominations spread their faith to Africa, Asia, and the Americas, where communities frequently adapted their teachings and rituals to local social and cultural ways. The spread of European settler colonies also greatly facilitated the diffusion of Christianity in the temperate regions. Islam and Buddhism took advantage of railroad and steamship technology to expand into new regions, partly in connection with the migrations of Asian and African workers. Pilgrims traveled in larger numbers than ever

> **The advance of secular culture challenged the world's religions, but, even so, most of the major faiths grew at a faster pace than ever.**

to holy sites—Roman Catholics to Rome, Muslims to Mecca, Hindus to the banks of the Ganges—where they identified intellectually and emotionally with a larger community of co-believers.

Opposition to rapid change, liberal practices, and European colonialism often took religious form. Christian, Jewish, Muslim, Hindu, and Confucian leaders protested foreign rule and growing social inequalities in their lands. Numerous sects arose to preach millenarianism, a word related to "millennium" and referring to a "thousand years" of justice on earth. Millenarian ideology centered on the idea that supernatural forces would bring about a sudden change to end foreign domination, social inequality, and even all evil. Millenarian movements included the Ghost Dance religion of American Indians on the Great Plains, the Tai'ping Rebellion in China, and the appearance of the Mahdi in the Muslim Sudan, an individual divinely inspired to establish a "reign of peace." Ultimately, none of these movements withstood the power of modern weaponry.

> By 1914, the notion that humans could be conceived as property was broadly condemned, and slavery itself legally abolished throughout much of the world. The fact that industrialists and commercial farmers continued to substitute other forms of coerced labor for slavery, and that the struggle against slavery continues today, does not detract from this achievement.

Liberal, Democratic, and Nationalist Ideas Around the World

Outside Europe, debates over reform and progress pursued complex paths. In countries as diverse as Turkey, Russia, Mexico, and China the supporters of economic reforms stressed the benefits of liberal economic improvement. However, because these reforms tended to make economic inequalities worse, they had little popular appeal, leading to counter-movements in support of those impoverished by change. Also, traditional elites such as landowners, church officials, and high-ranking military officers saw these changes as undermining their way of life and therefore resolved to resist them.

The ideology of the Atlantic revolutions had profound influence on political reform movements. In many ways struggles over these ideas continue to this day. At the beginning of the era, slavery was broadly accepted and widely practiced. By 1914, the notion that humans could be conceived as property was broadly condemned, and slavery itself legally abolished throughout much of the world. The fact that industrialists and commercial farmers continued to substitute other forms of coerced labor for slavery, and that the struggle against slavery continues today, does not detract from this achievement.

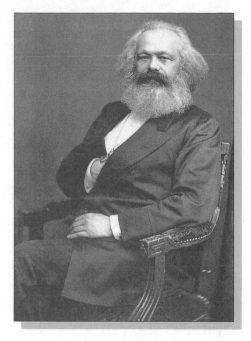

Karl Marx, 1818–1883. He authored *The Communist Manifesto.*

At the start of the era, the holders of power almost everywhere in the world viewed the notion of popular sovereignty, that is, that people are citizens, not subjects, and should have the right to vote and hold office, as dangerous nonsense. By 1914, the principle that the right to govern belongs to the people and not to a divinely appointed monarch, was deeply engrained in the industrialized countries. The struggle for the enfranchisement of women also got underway, though it made much greater gains in the early twentieth century.

A third transforming idea was that workers have rights, among them the right to organize to advance their economic and social interests. In Big Era Seven, workers' rights gradually gained momentum in industrialized countries. A major stimulus to worker organization was the philosophy of Karl Marx, whose *Communist Manifesto* (1848) presented an alternative vision of history centered on the interests of the working class. Marx's writings, together with those of other socialist authors, had their roots in the ideas of the European Enlightenment and the Atlantic revolutions, but they also offered a critique of liberal reform and its failure to address inequality.

Finally, there was nationalism, one of the greatest forces contributing to the modern revolution. Although we see the world today as self-evidently divided into nations, this was not always so. In 1750, monarchy was the prevailing form of government, while language and ethnicity, though important, were not viewed as the proper basis on which to organize states. Individuals were subjects and not citizens. By 1914, things had changed dramatically. Most people in Europe and the Americas widely accepted the nationalist principle that a "people" defined by shared language, culture, and history had a natural right to govern themselves. Nationalism sought to convince individuals to merge their hopes and dreams with those of the "imagined community" of the nation, that is, a community that had distinctive cultural characteristics in common but whose members did not for the most part know one another. The rise of nationalist thought was linked to growing literacy and public education. It was also connected to the mechanization of printing, the growth of a market for printed works, and the diffusion of newspapers and other print materials by way of the new communication technologies. Generally, the leaders of states encouraged nationalism, proclaiming that the interests of the state and the nation were one. Nationalism was therefore a potential antidote to social divisions within a society: wealthy capitalists, middle classes, and the laboring poor should subordinate their economic differences and conflicts to common loyalty to the nation-state. In the later nineteenth century, nationalist ideas became an important factor in politics in such places as the Ottoman empire, the Austrian empire, Egypt, China, India, and South Africa.

The modern revolution involved not only economic and political changes but a profound cultural upheaval. It reshaped our understandings of the natural world and the place of humans in it, our basic economic and political understandings, and our sense of cultural identity. Today, we are conscious that the modern world is radically different from all earlier eras.

CHAPTER 7 STUDY QUESTIONS

1. What single characteristic do you think most clearly describes the modern revolution, that is, the coming of modernity? Explain your choice. What do you think are some of the factors that distinguish the modern world we live in today from the world of Big Eras One–Six?

2. What aspects of the modern revolution contributed to wider gaps in economic well-being and standards of living between different regions of the world? Why do you think these gaps became wider in Big Era Seven?

3. What features of life characterized industrial societies as of Big Era Seven's end? What elements had to be present to qualify a society as "industrial?" If you lived in 1900, would you have preferred to live in a big industrial city or in a village in the countryside? What might have been the advantages and disadvantages of living in one or the other?

4. What economic and social connections might you describe, if any, between the Industrial Revolution and large-scale, long-distance migrations in the nineteenth century?

5. In the eighteenth and nineteenth centuries, many people proclaimed their desire for liberty and equality. What sort of people gained greater liberty and equality? What people did not? What do you think liberty and equality meant to people in those two centuries? What do they mean to you today?

Big Era Eight

A Half-Century of Crises, 1900–1945 CE

By the end of the nineteenth century, societies around the globe had been brought within a single, rapidly evolving world system as a result of what we called in the previous chapter the modern revolution. This system linked different regions and peoples economically, politically, and culturally. Within this system, some states and groups accumulated colossal wealth and power, while others fell into economic and political decline.

The world system was dominated by the industrialized states of Europe, which had been weak and marginal powers just a few centuries before. In the nineteenth century, however, rapid industrialization gave European states colossal economic and military power. By 1910, they ruled India and most of Africa and Southeast Asia. Japan controlled Korea and Taiwan, and the United States held the Philippines. Other states, such as China, the Ottoman empire, and several republics of Latin America, fell within the sphere of economic and political influence of one or more of these powers. Still other regions, including North America, parts of Latin America, Siberia, and Australasia had been largely settled by immigrants of European origin. European settler minorities dominated South Africa and Algeria. European culture and science, as well as a characteristically European faith in progress and reason, also exerted a powerful influence outside Europe. Those ideas were particularly attractive to elite groups who wanted to modernize their own societies.

Where industrialization did not take place, integration into the world system often meant greater economic weakness. China, Persia, and the Ottoman empire, for example, lost much of the economic clout they experienced in the world between the sixteenth and eighteenth centuries. At the same time, peasants and artisans throughout the world found it harder to compete in international markets against manufacturers and farmers in industrialized regions, who enjoyed the advantages of high productivity and government protection of their interests.

Early in the twentieth century, rapid economic and technological change, increasing competition among powerful states, and resistance to European domination worked together to destabilize the world system. Underlying tensions and weaknesses led to a series of crises that altered the world in several important ways:

- Rapid economic growth put increasing pressure on the natural environment.

- A return to economic protectionism expressed chiefly in high tariffs for imports undermined global economic integration.

- Two world wars, which unleashed terrible weapons such as the atomic bomb backed by the power of industrial production, devastated Europe, Japan, and other combat zones, and helped undermine European wealth and power.

- Countries with rising economies, notably the United States, Japan, and the Soviet Union, began to challenge Europe's economic power.

- Anti-colonial and nationalist movements began to weaken Europe's grip on its colonies and spheres of influence.

- In the sciences and arts, new theories, attitudes, and insights eroded the confidence of late nineteenth-century European thinkers. The horrors of global war provoked new ways of looking at the world and a search for new ideas beyond Europe. At the same time, new technologies of mass communication brought to prominence a modern mass culture that was no longer the preserve of elites.

Despite these wrenching changes, the industrialized regions of Europe, North America, the USSR, and Japan, which accounted together for about 75 percent of the globe's Gross Domestic Product (GDP), still dominated the system. But it was now split into competing blocs headed by two new superpowers, the U.S. and the USSR. The confident faith in progress, reason, and enlightened liberal government that had dominated the thought of educated people in the later nineteenth century was now gone.

HUMANS AND THE ENVIRONMENT

New technologies and rapid population growth increased the impact of human societies on the natural environment, with consequences that varied greatly from region to region. Population trends that had started in Big Era Seven continued after 1900. Between 1913 and 1950, the number of humans rose from 1.8 billion to 2.5 billion, despite huge losses caused by warfare, genocide, disease, and pollution. Rates of growth were relatively slow in Europe, China, and India, and faster in other parts of Asia and in Latin America and Africa. Food production rose as farmers brought more and more virgin land into cultivation and built more complex irrigation systems. One huge advance of the late nineteenth century was the knowledge of how to chemically synthesize ammonia, which involved extracting nitrogen from the air. The chemical fertilizers that this process made possible revolutionized agricultural production in the twentieth century.

Clearer understanding of how diseases worked led in the late nineteenth century to vaccinations for smallpox, typhoid, and other viral diseases. Increased food production, improved medicine and sanitation, and a decline in the virulence and frequency of pandemic diseases such as plague, explain why global death rates fell and life expectancies rose from 31 to 49 years. This increase in human life span counts as one of the most fundamental changes of the modern revolution. Yet, as death rates declined, birth rates in much of the world remained as high as ever. The widening gap between static birth rates and falling death rates explains why populations grew faster than ever before.

> Yet, as death rates declined, birth rates in much of the world remained as high as ever. The widening gap between static birth rates and falling death rates explains why populations grew faster than ever before.

The Shift to Cities

Rapid population growth drove many types of environmental changes. The populations and physical areas of cities grew immensely. Between 1913 and 1950, the percentage of the world's population living in towns and cities rose from about 18 percent to almost 30 percent. Levels of urbanization, however, varied greatly from region to region. By 1950, more than 50 percent of people in the most industrialized countries lived in cities, about 40 percent in Latin America and the USSR, and less than 20 percent in the least industrialized regions, including China, South Asia, and much of Africa.

Migration, partly from rural areas to cities and partly from Europe to North America, southern South America, and Australasia, spurred rapid urban growth. Between 1914 and 1949, more than seven million people migrated to the United States, Canada, Australia, and New Zealand. The rapid growth of cities also reflected a fundamental change in the relationship between urban and rural areas. For thousands of years, death rates had typically been higher in towns than in villages. However, the introduction of improved sanitation and better treatments for epidemic diseases pushed urban death rates below those in the countryside for the first time in human history.

Change in Percent of Population Living in Cities[12]

Region	1890	1950
USA	35	64
Japan	30	56
China	5	11
Western Europe	35	63
Latin America	5	41
Africa	5	15
World	14	29

For each of these six regions, calculate the percentage of population growth between 1890 and 1950. What factors might help account for differences in these percentages?

The French impressionist artist Claude Monet's 1904 painting of the British Parliament in London shows the sun partially blocked by the city's smog-laden atmosphere.

Humans Reshaping the Environment

As populations grew, towns and cities gobbled up surrounding countryside, and the expansion of farmlands and pastures cut ever deeper into forests and grassy steppes. Deforestation was particularly rapid in tropical regions, as foresters felled timber to supply local and international demand, and farmers cleared land for cash crops such as coffee. Land erosion was another growing problem, particularly where migrant farmers tilled soils that were more fragile than they understood. This was the case with the creation of the "dust bowl" in the United States in the 1930s. Animal species suffered on land and sea. The total fish catch rose from about 2 million tons in 1900 to about 15 million tons in 1950. Consequently, fisheries from the North Sea to the Pacific began to collapse.

The spread of technologies pioneered in Big Era Seven magnified the individual's average environmental impact because men and women consumed more energy and resources while producing more waste. People used more and more coal, but oil production rose even faster to generate electricity and to feed the new internal combustion engines that widely replaced steam engines. Waste

> **Between 1913 and 1950, the world's total GDP almost doubled, while output per person rose by almost 50 percent.**

products from the burning of fossil fuels reduced air quality, particularly in big cities such as London and Chicago. In the course of the era, millions may have died from the effects of air pollution.

Between 1913 and 1950, the world's total GDP almost doubled, while output per person rose by almost 50 percent. Near the end of the era, humans acquired a new source of energy, nuclear power. This source was so potent that, in theory, it gave humans the ability to destroy much of the biosphere within a few hours. For better or worse, human impact on the environment increased more sharply in this era than ever before. Indeed, humans became a major force for change in the biosphere. This is why some scientists now argue that we have entered the "Anthropocene," a new geological area in which humans are the most important single force shaping the biosphere.

HUMANS AND OTHER HUMANS

Between 1900 and 1945, the world changed drastically. Global economic growth slowed. Powerful states fragmented into competing blocs. Communist, anti-capitalist states were established in the former Russian and Chinese empires. Anti-colonial movements emerged in Europe's colonies. Economic, military, and political power began to shift away from Europe towards the United States, Japan, and the Soviet Union.

The Economic Roller Coaster

Between 1870 and 1913, the global economy had grown at the unprecedented rate of 2.11 percent per annum. Between 1913 and 1950, growth slowed to 1.85 percent, then rose again to 4.91 percent from 1950 to 1973.[13] International trade also declined in Big Era Eight as the global commercial system splintered. Between 1913 and 1950, the proportion of world production that was traded internationally actually fell, so that in 1950 it was less than it had been in 1870.

Part of the problem was that as productivity soared in the late nineteenth century and producers found it harder to market surplus goods, the major trading nations became increasingly protectionist, that is, they imposed or raised import duties. Protectionism encouraged global rivalry for markets and colonies. In fact, World War I (1914–1918) was fought, in part, for global market share. Production revived after the war, but so did the pre-war problem of finding markets for surpluses. Other factors made the competition vicious, especially between the European industrial and naval rivals Britain and Germany. The huge costs of the war, together with the determination of the victors to make Germany and Austria pay reparations, led to an international trading and finance system that depended on a complicated and unstable system of international loans. American bankers loaned money to Germany to pay off its British and French creditors, who were also indebted to American bankers.

When those bankers began pulling their money back, the global economic system crashed. Industrial output, farm production, and employment plummeted. The effects of the "Crash of 1929" were particularly severe in the more industrialized regions, including Europe, North America, and Japan. But declining demand in those regions also hurt producers of rubber, minerals, and other raw materials in Latin America, Africa, and much of Asia. For a time, it seemed that, as Marx had predicted, the entire capitalist system was on the verge of collapse. Most governments reacted by cutting expenditures and raising import barriers, which further disrupted the economic system.

Eventually, many governments realized that they could spend their way out of the Great Depression. Government spending stimulated employment by putting cash into the pockets of wage earners, who in turn bought more consumer goods, raising production. In the U.S., the "New Deal," the economic policy of President Franklin Roosevelt, pumped millions into the economy through government programs mostly designed to build new infrastructure and provide employment. Between 1914 and 1938, governments of industrialized countries took on economic roles never before seen in history. In France, Germany, Japan, Britain, and the United States between 1913 and 1938, government expenditure rose as a percentage of total GDP from about 12 percent to about 28 percent. In the USSR in the 1930s, the government seized control of the entire economy. The U.S., the Soviet Union, and Japan all emerged as major economic and military powers, and by the end of the era, Europe was no longer the dominant center of strong growth. Comparative growth rates tell the story *(see table on next page)*.

Gross Domestic Product (GDP)
Average Annual Growth Rate Percentages, 1913–1950[14]

Eastern Europe	1.14
Western Europe	1.19
Soviet Union	2.15
Japan	2.44
United States	2.84
Latin America	3.43

What factors might help account for the differences in annual GDP growth rates in these six regions between 1913 and 1950?

The most powerful growth stimulator, however, turned out to be rearmament for war. By the late 1930s, all the major economic powers, including Japan and the U.S., as well as European states, were engaged in massive arms buildups. This fueled growth, but it also reawakened old rivalries.

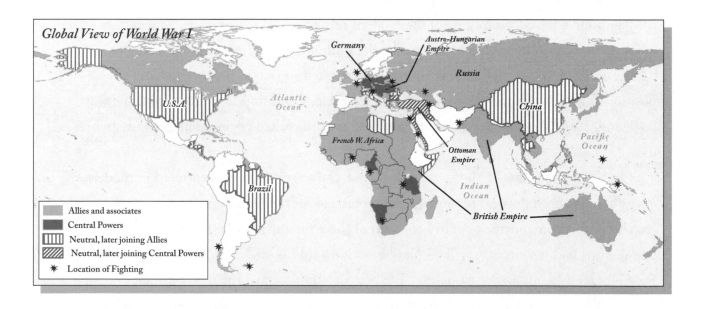

Global View of World War I

Germany
Austro-Hungarian Empire
Russia
China
Atlantic Ocean
U.S.A.
Ottoman Empire
French W. Africa
Brazil
Indian Ocean
Pacific Ocean
British Empire

Allies and associates
Central Powers
Neutral, later joining Allies
Neutral, later joining Central Powers
✳ Location of Fighting

The Great War

The two world wars together were a major cause of change in the global distribution of power. The wars had many causes, including competition for markets and colonies and a centuries-old tradition of military competition among European countries. In the late nineteenth century, the major industrialized states used their increasing economic and technological power to build up stocks of modern weapons such as machine guns

German stormtroops training in a dummy trench system near Sedan,
France, May 1917

and battleships. They also prepared for war by forging alliances that committed each country to the defense of its allies. The dangers of this system became apparent when Archduke Francis Ferdinand, the heir to the throne of the Austro-Hungarian empire, was assassinated by a Serbian nationalist in June 1914. Austro-Hungary consequently invaded Serbia, Serbia's ally Russia mobilized against Austro-Hungary, and within weeks the whole of Europe was embroiled in war.

World War I proved more horrifying than anyone could have imagined, and it demonstrated the colossal destructive power available to industrialized states. The conflagration showed a dark side of the modern revolution. Machine guns, long-range artillery, and mustard gas killed soldiers by the millions. Aircraft strafed and dropped bombs on soldiers and civilians. These weapons worked so well in holding defensive positions that decisive attacks were almost impossible. On Europe's western front the war settled into a grisly, prolonged siege in which soldiers assaulted enemy trenches only to be mowed down.

On the home fronts of all the states involved, the huge power concentrated in modern governments and industrial economies was harnessed for the fight. Warfare became "total," as governments took control of much of the economy in order to mobilize their populations and resources. Civilians played as vital a role as soldiers and also accounted for an increasing number of casualties. The war also transformed the lives of many women, who had to manage all aspects of domestic life when men were away and who took over men's jobs in munitions factories and other branches of production.

Because the rivalries that caused the war were worldwide, so was its impact. The Ottoman Turkish empire joined World War I on the German and Austro-Hungarian side. French, British, or Japanese forces seized German colonies in the Pacific and Africa. Troops from French and British colonies in Asia and Africa, and from former colonies such as Canada, Australia, and New Zealand fought on the British and French side.

In 1917, the U.S. entered the war against Germany and its allies. U.S. supplies, troops, and money, together with the huge economic and agricultural resources of the British and French empires, eventually tipped the balance against the central European powers. On November 11, 1918, Germany signed an armistice.

By then, 15 million soldiers had died and another 20 million had been injured. Millions of civilians died as well, and destruction of infrastructure, industries, and farmland was colossal. The end of the war left the liberal capitalist system facing many daunting challenges.

The Paris Peace Conference (1919) stripped Germany of its colonies and saddled it and Austria with the burden of paying reparations, which included much of the cost of the war. It also created the League of Nations, the first fledgling world deliberative body, whose primary mission was to prevent future military catastrophes. The League had little independent power, however, and the punitive peace treaty of 1919 ensured that Germany and Austria would continue to nurse resentments.

The Rise of the Soviet Union

Vladimir Lenin, Marxist leader of the Bolsheviks

In Russia the creation of the world's first communist state posed a challenge to the entire capitalist system, a challenge that would last until the 1990s. In the late nineteenth century, the Russian empire tried hard to industrialize to keep up with the rest of Europe. However, the strains of rapid economic change combined with the war, which saw a German invasion, undermined the autocratic government of Tsar Nicholas II. In February 1917, he was forced to abdicate and to leave the country in the hands of a weak "provisional government." Into this political vacuum stepped the Bolshevik Party, led by Vladimir Lenin (1870–24). As a Marxist, Lenin had no use for nineteenth century-style liberalism, and he was convinced that the war signaled the collapse of both capitalism and imperialism. He believed that Russia would pioneer a new and better type of society, one that would do away with the political and economic inequalities of the capitalist world order.

The Bolsheviks unilaterally pulled Russia out of the war, won a civil struggle against internal enemies, and expelled most of the country's capitalists. They were left, however, ruling a country, now the Union of Soviet Socialist Republics, that was poorer and less industrialized than it had been ten years earlier. Before they could realize communism, they argued, they would have to rebuild Russia's economy. In 1929, Stalin, Lenin's successor, launched a radical, state-led industrialization drive. He used planning techniques pioneered by wartime governments and much of the technology invented in the nineteenth and early twentieth centuries, from railways to radios. He ruthlessly seized Russian peasant lands, thereby eliminating the last remaining bastions of capitalism.

The strains and costs of compulsory industrialization were great, including a massive famine, creation of forced labor camps, and political purges that by the 1930s cost the lives of several million people. Even so, Stalin's brutal methods produced a powerful industrial economy. This success inspired some political leaders and revolutionaries in other lands, including western European countries and their colonies, to take up the communist vision of the future. Though communist movements made little headway in most places, communist leader Mao Zedong achieved victory in China. On October 1, 1949, he announced the formation of the "People's Republic of China." This meant that about one-third of all humans lived under communist governments.

Fascist Governments

In Germany, Adolph Hitler's ideology of "National Socialism" (Nazism) offered a second authoritarian alternative to liberal democracy. Nazism built on the sense of despair that World War I, the Depression, and the punitive war reparations caused among Germans. Nazism offered an extreme version of the competitive nationalist ideologies that had led to the war. Hitler became an advocate of fascism, an ideology that saw politics in terms of racial conflict between different nations, championed authoritarianism, and despised liberal values. The Nazi party flourished, and in 1933 Hitler became Germany's leader. Exploiting international disunity and the weakness of the League of Nations, which the United States never joined, Germany threw off the Versailles Treaty's penalties and restrictions and began to rearm. As in other countries, huge government expenditure for weapons was just the stimulus needed to revive the German economy. This in turn boosted Hitler's popularity. Benito Mussolini (1883–1945), Hitler's fascist ally in Italy, embarked on a similar program of nationalist rearmament. Fascism found other imitators as well, for example, in Spain, Brazil, and Lebanon.

Nationalism in the Colonized World

In colonized regions of the world, nationalist leaders began to challenge European control, many inspired by the liberal democratic traditions of Europe and the U.S.,

some inspired by communism and fascism. World War I destroyed the empires of Germany, Austria, and Ottoman Turkey. Germany's colonies and Ottoman territory in the Middle East were taken over by France and Britain as "mandates" or "trusteeships" theoretically under the League of Nations. (The German colony of Southwest Africa was turned over to South Africa as a mandate.) Consequently, the British and French empires not only

Mustafa Kemal Ataturk (1881–1938), the Turkish military officer who led Turkey to independence in 1921

survived the war but became even bigger. However, Turkey, the heartland of the former Ottoman empire, emerged from the war as an independent state under the leadership of Mustafa Kemal Ataturk.

Nevertheless, nationalist movements for reform and independence began to come together in the colonies. In India, the Indian National Congress, first established in 1885, became a powerful supporter of independence. In Mohandas Gandhi (1869–1948) it found an inspirational and creative leader. His non-violent protests against British rule played a crucial role in achieving independence in 1947. In parts of Africa, too, new educated leaders, including Kwame Nkrumah, Leopold Senghor, and Julius Nyerere, emerged, and in the aftermath of World War II they began to demand total independence. In China and Vietnam the anti-imperial rhetoric of Soviet communism provided the inspiration for the nationalist leaders Mao Zedong and Ho Chi Minh. In all those regions, intellectuals, artists, and politicians wrestled with the fundamental fact that the modern revolution had arrived in the form of European colonialism, unfavorable trade relations, and European ideas of progress. These women and men were determined to advance modern technology, science, and political organization but equally set on finding ways to do it that were true to their own national traditions and aspirations.

Challenges to Democracies

The major liberal democracies were by no means immune to new problems. Governments were pressed to take their own liberal rhetoric more seriously by extending the vote to larger sections of the population and to women as well as men. New Zealand granted the vote to women in 1893, the first sovereign state to do so. The United States and most European countries followed only after World War I. Socialist parties also challenged governments, particularly during the Great Depression, to tackle the inequalities that were still widespread in democratic and wealthy nations.

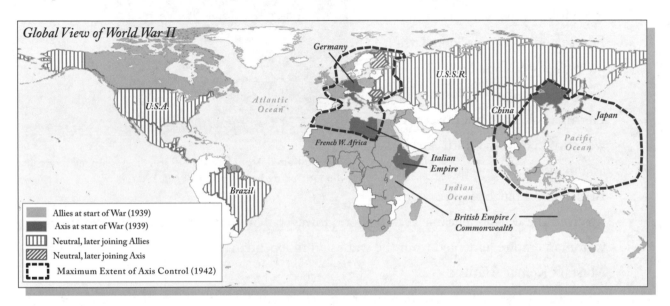

Global View of World War II

- Allies at start of War (1939)
- Axis at start of War (1939)
- Neutral, later joining Allies
- Neutral, later joining Axis
- Maximum Extent of Axis Control (1942)

World War II

All the challenges of the 1920s and 1930s led toward a new round of conflict. In some sense, World War II was a continuation of the first war. Japan, seeking to create its own empire in East Asia, invaded Chinese Manchuria in 1931 and mainland China in 1937. Fascist Italy invaded Ethiopia in 1935. In Europe, Nazi racist belligerence and aggression against its neighbors, first Austria and Czechoslovakia, then Poland, led Germany in 1939 into war with France and Britain.

The conflict soon became global. Germany attacked the Soviet Union in 1941, and Japan, Hitler's ally, attacked the United States at Pearl Harbor, Hawaii, on December 7, 1941. World War II was fought in Europe, the Soviet Union, North Africa, West Africa, East Asia, Southeast Asia, and the Atlantic and Pacific oceans. Eventually, the sheer weight of resources and human numbers ranged against the fascist alliance made the difference. Britain and France fought with the support of both soldiers and civilians from colonies and former colonies throughout the world. The U.S. concentrated its wealth, industry, and citizenry on the war effort. And the Soviet Union mobilized huge human and material resources with brutal efficiency. The Allied Powers invaded Germany from both east and west in 1945, and Hitler died in his Berlin bunker. Japan surrendered after the U.S. dropped atomic bombs on Hiroshima and Nagasaki in August. The Hiroshima attack killed perhaps 80,000 people, and it ended the war with Japan.

Newly liberated from the Buchenwald concentration camp, a Soviet prisoner of war identifies a former security guard known for savagely beating the prisoners. Do you think this photo is an informative representation of Nazi imprisonment policies or of the Holocaust? Why or why not?

In human terms, World War II was even more costly than the first conflict. Perhaps 60 million people died, or 3 percent of the world's population. This time, most of the casualties were civilians. Weapons such as bombers and rockets brought warfare into the centers of cities. Mobilization for war was even more "total" than in the first war, particularly in Germany and the Soviet Union. The horror of the war found its most potent symbol in the Nazis' systematic murder of 9 million people, 6 million of them Jews.

HUMANS AND IDEAS

Despite crisis after crisis, Big Era Eight brought new creativity to science, the arts, popular culture, and political and social thought. Communism, fascism, and new liberation movements opposed to European imperialism severely challenged the liberal ideologies of Europe and the United States. Even for many citizens of European democracies, the horrors of war seemed to discredit the liberal ideology that had seemed so full of promise in the late nineteenth century. The historian Oswald Spengler, for example, captured this mood in a work called *The Decline of the West*, which he first published in 1918. The book, which became a bestseller, argued that all civilizations rise and fall and that World War I marked the beginning of Europe's decline. To many, liberalism seemed only a veneer that protected exploitative and incompetent governments and allowed social and economic inequities in the world to continue. On the other hand, the U.S., Britain, and several other European countries mobilized millions of citizens for war without compromising their democratic institutions very much. In fact, these nations broadened the base of popular participation in civic life, notably to include women.

Science and Art

The challenges to nineteenth-century traditions extended to science and the arts. Albert Einstein, Werner Heisenberg, and other scientists developed the theory of relativity and quantum physics in the first three decades of the twentieth century. They both undermined Isaac Newton's model of a fixed and predictable universe, which scientists of the nineteenth century had taken for granted. In psychology, Sigmund Freud showed the power of irrational forces that lurked in the human subconscious. In the fine arts, a mood of anti-rationalism and pessimism brought forth new genres of art. More extensive cross-cultural exchanges of artistic ideas challenged established artistic traditions in most parts of the world. For example, West African wood sculpture inspired the Spanish painter Pablo Picasso (1881–1973), and Mongolian artists incorporated traditional motifs into contemporary art forms such as photography. Entirely new art forms, such as motion pictures, radio drama, and jazz blurred the lines between elite and popular culture.

> The challenges to nineteenth-century traditions extended to science and the arts.

Mass Communication and Popular Culture

Perhaps for the first time in history, popular culture, instead of being just the cultural heritage of a particular region, began to reach around the globe. Soviet leaders deliberately used cinema to spread their socialist message to rural villages. In doing so, however, they also ensured that Soviet movie-goers would learn about Hollywood and American values. Radios gave leaders access to vast audiences, and gifted speakers such as Roosevelt, Hitler, and Churchill used the new medium to mobilize whole nations for war. The popular press helped spread new political messages, including fascism and communism, while giving people in democratic societies broader and quicker access to information about the world. Nationalist leaders in Africa, the Middle East, and Asia became increasingly skilled at using newspapers and radio to build mass support. The new media also helped popularize sports such as football and baseball. Refined cultural tastes and values, once the preserve of elite groups, spread increasingly among the working masses.

The world of 1950 was very different from the world of 1900. It was a world disillusioned with nineteenth-century hopes for progress, no longer politically and economically dominated by Western Europe, more populous, more urbanized, and more productive. The world of 1950, however, was just as divided and conflict-ridden, and it bristled with dangerous weapons unimaginable in 1900. In the aftermath of World War II, it was not at all certain that humans could find a way of living with the terrifying technological powers unleashed by the Industrial Revolution. Could peace be preserved better in the second half of the century? Could the machinery of economic growth reduce the global inequalities that had helped fuel the conflicts of 1900–1950? Or was the world doomed to ever more destructive conflicts as power groups fought over the wealth that the technology and science of the modern revolution had generated?

Franklin Roosevelt leads a radio broadcasted "fireside chat" in Washington, D.C.

CHAPTER 8 STUDY QUESTIONS

1. Do you think World War I was avoidable? Why or why not?

2. What were major shared characteristics of fascism, Nazism, and communism? How were these ideologies different from each other? Compare these ideologies with Liberalism as defined in the nineteenth century. How would you explain the popular appeal of fascism, Nazism, and communism in the 1920s and 1930s?

3. Compare Big Era Eight with previous Big Eras in terms of the impact that humans had on the physical and natural environment. How do you think the world wars contributed to environmental change?

4. How would you account for the greatly-increased involvement of many governments in their countries' economies in the twentieth century? What are some of the ways that governments intervened in and regulated economic life in Big Era Eight?

5. During Big Era Eight, women gained the right to vote in many countries. Why do you think women had voting rights in so few countries before the twentieth century? Why did a large change occur in Big Era Eight?

Big Era Nine

Paradoxes of Global Acceleration, 1945–Present

Big Era Nine is different from earlier eras in that we do not yet know where it is leading. Nevertheless, we can distinguish some key world historical processes that have been especially important in shaping the current era. Their interactions, sometimes unforeseen, have given rise to major new challenges to humanity. Others as yet unknown lie in the future. Here we can at least suggest some key trends to watch:

- Human population has reached 6.4 billion, shattering all previous records and posing major challenges for the future. Already more than 50 percent of humans live in cities, a trend that seems certain to increase. The basic demographic patterns raise major questions about how to feed, clothe, house, and provide meaningful lives for so many people. They also pose significant environmental questions.

- The environmental effects of human actions have accumulated drastically during this era. Already manifest in previous Big Eras, environmental damage since 1950 has become progressively more severe and widespread. In some areas, it has become potentially irreversible. It includes massive deforestation, land degradation, atmospheric pollution, the extinction of species, the fouling of the world's oceans and rivers, and global warming. For the first time, anthropogenic (that is, human generated) environmental change threatens the future of our species, if not the entire planet.

- The ability of humans to extract more energy and resources from a given area of the earth has decisively increased during Big Era Nine. A key feature of this era has been the accelerating use of petroleum and natural gas, the continuation of a trend that began with the fossil fuel revolution in the eighteenth century (Big Era Seven). Petroleum, natural gas, coal, and, to a much lesser extent, atomic power have vastly increased the amount of energy for human use, even as some parts of the world continue to enjoy disproportionate access to it.

- Politically, the period witnessed the Cold War (1947–1989) and its aftermath, the rise of the United States to global dominance, and the end of European colonial empires in Asia and Africa. The world has been affected by great political turbulence and wars in which the risk of nuclear confrontation has been present. The period has also seen the founding of the United Nations and numerous international political and economic structures, for example, the World Bank.

- Since 1950, the global economy has grown faster than ever before in history. Indeed, by some measures, more economic growth has occurred in this era than in all previous eras of human history combined. Yet the ability of economic globalization to deliver better lives for all has been deeply compromised by its contradictions, especially boom and bust cycles and wider social inequality. Is it possible to develop a more just as well as a more productive and profitable global economy? The record so far is not encouraging.

- New technologies of transportation and communication have made it possible not only to link all parts of the world in real time but also to connect individuals more intimately and inexpensively via mobile phones, chat rooms, texting, and group websites. Thanks to the new electronic technologies of this era, governments and corporations have acquired unprecedented capacities to intervene in the lives of citizens, the better to observe, document, control, and organize multiple aspects of life. For better or worse, humans have been forced into closer interdependence than ever before.

- The continued escalation in the costs of military technology and its increasing development have made warfare vastly expensive for all states. Simultaneously, the costs of basic administrative, educational, and welfare services to unprecedented numbers of people have driven many states in the less developed world to the brink of collapse. In the gap between the capacity of states to organize and the growing global instability have come all sorts of private mercenaries, terror groups, and criminal syndicates. The race between order and disorder can be observed widely around the world.

In sum, the world has become increasingly contradictory and paradoxical. For some, rapid economic growth and globalization have offered opportunities. For others they have meant the destruction of cherished lifeways and ancient traditions. While many people got wealthier, many more experienced declining standards of living, nutrition, and health. The varied and often contradictory impact of change explains why Big Era Nine has been an era of constant military, political, and cultural conflict.

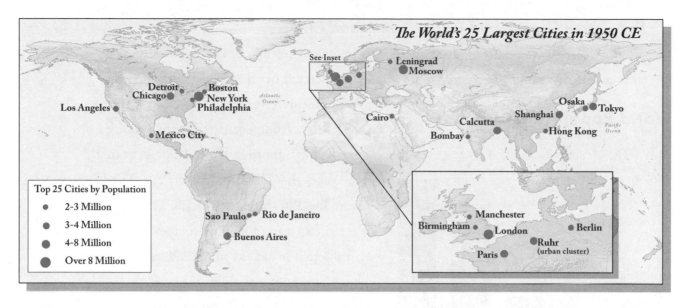

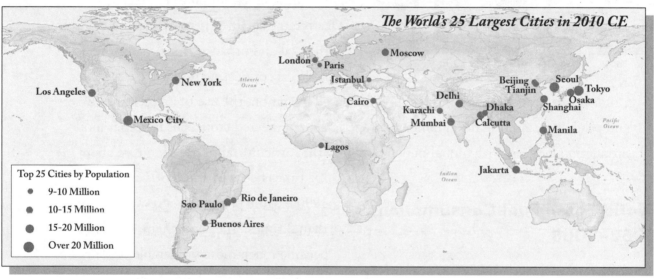

How would you account for the changes in the locations of the top cities in the world between 1950 and 2010?

HUMANS AND THE ENVIRONMENT

The single most important development in this era has been the scale of potentially irreversible human impact on the environment. This is an inevitable consequence of the staggering increase in global population from 2.5 billion in 1950 to more than 6 billion in 2000.

Population Growth and Its Environmental Effects

Between 1955 and 1990, average life expectancies throughout the world also rose from about 35 years to 55 years. Approximately 6 percent of all the humans who ever lived on earth were alive between 1950 and 2000. And because of increased life expectancy, approximately 12 percent of all the years that all humans have ever lived were lived in those fifty years.

World Population in Billions

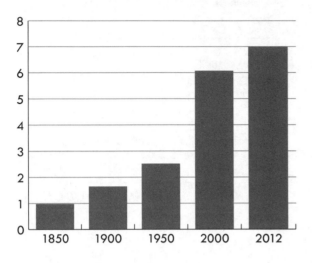

The spread of new medicines such as antibiotics as well as improved sanitation and health care, especially in the world's burgeoning cities, all played a role. Death rates declined throughout the world in both rural and urban regions, with some notable exceptions, such as the ex-Soviet Union. Agricultural changes, including increased irrigation, the use of artificial fertilizers and pesticides, and the development of genetically-engineered crops, ensured that food production kept up with global population growth. Agricultural production rose about 2.7 times between the 1950s and the 1990s, while population grew a little more than 2 times. The food chain, however, became much more vulnerable to widespread failure through its overdependence on energy-intensive agricultural practices and the increased dependency on globe-spanning chains of supply.

World Fossil Fuel Consumption, 1950–2008

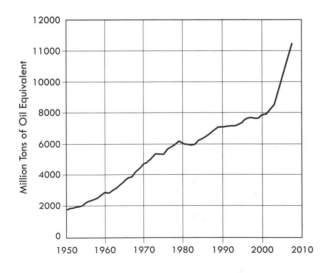

Unprecedented population growth has magnified human impact on forests, croplands, pastures, and seas. These effects have been particularly devastating in poorer countries, which lack resources to limit environmental damage. The spread of human populations has threatened many species with extinction by reducing the land and resources available to them. In 1996, about 20 percent of all vertebrate species on earth may have been in danger of extinction. In fact, the rate of extinctions today may be approaching the rates attained in the five or six eras of most rapid extinction over the past several hundred million years.

Colossal Energy Consumption and the Environment

Energy has been key to massive economic growth. Between 1950 and 2000, world energy consumption increased fourfold. The widespread use of petroleum and natural gas made unprecedented prosperity possible for some but also increased dependency upon non-renewable fossil fuels. Total world fossil fuel consumption increased from less than 2 billion tons in 1950 to 8 billion tons in 2000. With some notable exceptions, many parts of Africa and the global south, including Haiti, South Asia, and Brazil, continue to rely upon woodfires to cook meals, heat water, and warm homes.

New technologies have increased the scale and transformed the nature of environmental change. By 1990, roads and other spaces set aside for automobiles and trucks took up 5–10 percent of the total land surface in North America, Europe, and Japan, and about 1 percent in the world as a whole.[15] Modern transportation systems helped spread diseases such as AIDS, the SARS virus, and various types of influenza throughout the world within just a few years or even a few months. Scientists have

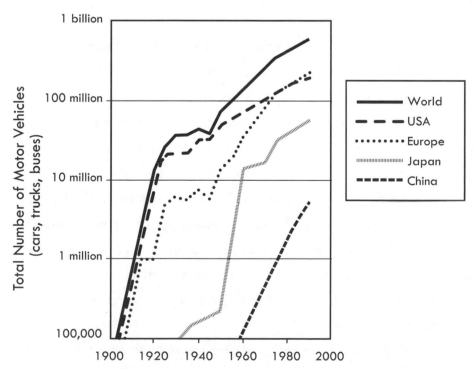

What factors might help explain the relative growth rate and number of motor vehicles in these four countries?

created thousands of new chemicals, from plastics to fertilizers to chlorofluorocarbons (CFC). Many of these substances are harmful to humans and animals. By the 1970s, the Rhine river carried such high levels of chromium, nickel, copper, zinc, and lead that a Dutch expert complained that the river was "metal-plating Holland."[16]

The second half of the twentieth century witnessed the end of European colonial empires and the rise to independence of many new countries.

Increasing use of fossil fuels, particularly coal and oil, has pumped such huge quantities of carbon dioxide and other "greenhouse gases" into the atmosphere that these gases threaten to raise average temperatures and thus transform global weather patterns. "Global warming," as this process is known, could have a devastating impact on low-lying areas, which are likely to be flooded as sea levels rise. Global warming may indeed transform the world's climate. Nuclear power, which many at first saw as a source of virtually limitless clean energy, has turned out to be costly and dangerous. Its waste products not only take thousands of years to decay but also provide the raw materials for new and terrible weapons. No credible waste disposal system has yet emerged. Nuclear bombs have given humans the power, if they choose, to destroy much of the biosphere within just a few hours. For the first time in planetary history, a single species has become a major force for change in the biosphere as a whole.

Though global in their scale, these environmental effects have differed from one region to another. Many of the wealthier industrialized nations have begun to reverse some forms of environmental damage by improving water and air, replanting forests, checking soil degradation in arid areas, and slowing the spread of infectious diseases. In dry and forest regions, however, farmers have often had to use the land in unsustainable ways merely to survive. Poorer countries have also found it harder to deal with diseases. The number of adults suffering from AIDS has been held below 1 percent in the U.S., but in some regions, the disease's impact has been far more devastating. In the mid-1990s, for example, almost one quarter of all adults in Zimbabwe, Botswana, Namibia, Swaziland, and Zambia had the HIV virus that causes AIDS. While many in richer countries have begun to see environmental degradation as a future danger, many in poorer regions already live with environmental crisis.

Global population growth has slowed since the 1960s because birth rates have fallen, particularly in the wealthiest and most urbanized regions. It now seems likely that human populations will level out at about 9 or 10 billion in the middle of the twenty-first century. In the long run, a slowing of demographic growth is bound to help reduce human impact on the environment. While the full consequences of humanity's rapidly increasing impact on the biosphere are not yet clear, humans began for the first time in Big Era Nine to grapple with environmental problems at a global level.

HUMANS AND OTHER HUMANS

The second half of the twentieth century witnessed the end of European colonial empires and the rise to independence of many new countries in Africa and Asia, as well as the establishment of major international organizations, including the United Nations, the World Court, the World Bank, and the International Monetary Fund. The era has also been marked by the rise to global power of the United States in the aftermath of World War II. Finally, the period largely coincided with the Cold War (1947–1989) and its aftermath.

It is also possible, however, to perceive emerging new constellations of political and economic power. The challenge of global population increase has intensified struggles over scarce resources (especially water and energy). The world economy, which enjoyed a half century of remarkable growth, has begun to display previously undetected vulnerabilities. By 2000, assertive new political actors, especially the European Union, China, and India, were beginning to provoke global power shifts. At the same time, the unraveling of states in tropical Africa and elsewhere has suggested that central governments can show themselves to be incapable of managing repeated political and economic crises.

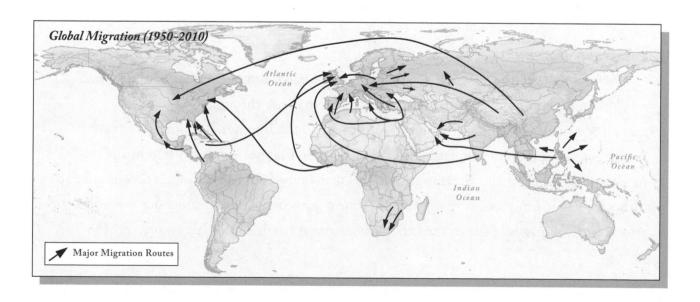

Global Migration (1950–2010)

Major Migration Routes

Big Science

The current era has seen the further expansion of the social phenomenon of "big science." Research and development have been increasingly organized by governments and large corporations and conducted in commercial laboratories, universities, and government research institutes. This trend got underway in the later nineteenth century. Both world wars, which created demand for new inventions and discoveries to solve particularly military and economic problems, greatly stimulated this trend. In the U.S., 40,000 people worked on the World War II Manhattan Project, whose goal was to create the first nuclear weapon. Many of the important technological innovations of Big Era Nine depended on such large research projects. They included the discovery of the structure of DNA (and its eventual decoding), the invention and development of microchips, and the systematic use of biotechnology in medicine and agriculture.

Global Migration

Another prominent feature of this era has been the mass movement of people around the globe. The availability of cheap air travel, improved rail and road grids, and the relaxing of laws restricting movements in and out of countries have made this surge possible, while the search for jobs and opportunities has largely motivated it. For example, almost 13 million migrants moved to North America and Australasia between 1950 and 1973 alone. In that same period, Caribbean islanders migrated to Britain, Turks to Germany, Senegalese to France, and Indians and Pakistanis to North America, Europe, and the Middle East. Chinese migrated to Xinjiang Province in the far west of the country and to Inner Mongolia. Russians moved to the steppes of Kazakhstan.

Electronic Communications

Perhaps more remarkable has been the impact of telecommunications and the digital revolution. By 2000, more than 1 billion phones were in use throughout the world, and several hundred million computers were linked to the Internet. The spread of mass media—newspapers, cinema, radio, television, and the Internet—ensured that images, news, and advertising also became global. Turkmen nomads in Inner Eurasia use satellite dishes to watch American soap operas, and young women and men throughout the world, responding to images of life in the U.S., began to wear baseball caps backwards. As the philosopher Marshall McLuhan predicted in the 1960s, the world seemed to be turning into a single "global village."

> The spread of mass media... ensured that images, news, and advertising also became global. As the philosopher Marshall McLuhan predicted in the 1960s, the world seemed to be turning into a single "global village."

Postwar Economic Growth and Trade

Globalization has been closely linked to economic growth. Between 1950 and 1973, global GDP grew almost 5 percent per year before falling to the still respectable rate of 3 percent after 1973. In just under fifty years, global GDP multiplied by more than six times. There were many causes of growth. The major capitalist powers deliberately engineered a revival of world trade after World War II, focusing primarily on Europe and Japan. The U.S. pumped huge amounts of money into the reconstruction of both regions, and the major states collaborated to create an international financial system linked to the United Nations via the Bretton Woods Accords (1944).

As a result, international trade revived rapidly after the war. The volume of goods traded on international markets, which had fallen between 1913 and 1950, tripled between 1950 and 1995. As rural workers migrated to towns and as more and more women took up paid employment, the number of wage earners grew by leaps and bounds. This was even true for a time in the communist world, where high rates of growth in the 1950s and 1960s depended mainly on government-led industrialization drives. Chinese growth rates rose from 2.9 percent per year between 1950 and 1973 to 6.4 percent for most of the 1990s.

The benefits of growth, however, have been distributed unevenly. Living standards rose most rapidly in the industrialized capitalist regions and to some extent in Russia and China but more slowly in much of the developing world. After the Great Depression, capitalist governments and producers learned how important it was to sustain demand by ensuring that consumers could keep buying things. The importance of mass markets for goods such as refrigerators, televisions, and cars first became apparent in the U.S. between the two world wars. After World War II, mass consumption of these and other goods also helped sustain growth in other capitalist economies, especially during the boom years before the 1970s. In the wealthier countries, rising living standards have also helped to defuse political radicalism and maintain the stability of democratic institutions.

For consumers in the richest nations, these changes have brought an unprecedented rise in living standards. In the world as a whole, however, economic differences between richer and poorer regions have become greater than ever, especially in the later 1970s, when the world economy slowed. The table below reveals these differences.

Per Capita Gross Income in 2011 (in $USD)

USA	48,147
10 countries of highest income (average)	62,427
Brazil	11,845
China	8,394
India	3,703
Liberia	416

What political, economic, social, or cultural factors might help account for the relative positions of these five countries in per capita gross income?

Economists in the wealthier regions kept insisting that eventually even the poorest areas would benefit from the dynamism of world capitalism. While China, Taiwan, South Korea, and India experienced industrial growth, this was not the case in much of Asia, Africa, and Latin America, which chiefly participated as sources of cheap raw materials. They gradually became deeply indebted to banks and governments in wealthier regions. By the 1970s world growth stagnated and even began to fall, particularly in parts of Africa and Latin America. Despite rapid world economic growth in the first part of the era, many were left behind. As late as 2002, 3 billion people had never used a telephone, and 1 billion people had no access to electricity.[17]

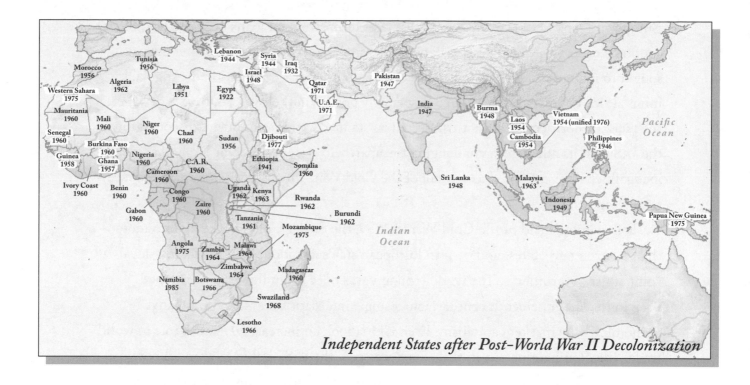

Independent States after Post–World War II Decolonization

The Cold War and Its End

During Big Era Nine, the Cold War (1944–1989) dominated world politics. This was a struggle in which many of the world's states clustered into one of two hostile blocs, one claiming to represent capitalism, the other communism. Fears of the spread of communism raised tensions throughout North America and Western Europe. In Russia, China, and Eastern Europe, communism sealed off a generation from the West, while facilitating state-led economic modernization. The Cold War also had a major impact upon the colonized territories of Asia, Africa, and Latin America, most of which obtained their independence in this era. Both of the power blocs sought out leaders of nationalist movements and new states to be their political clients, and they both supported propaganda wars to attack the beliefs and values of the other side. China, India, Cuba, Egypt, and many other countries benefited from Soviet aid, normally directed at large construction projects, for example, Egypt's Aswan dam on the Nile. While

Intercontinental ballistic missile (ICBM) Titan I launch

Europe and Japan benefited from massive U.S. reconstruction loans after the war, other countries experienced a stifling lack of progressive change as their big power patrons sought to maintain the status quo. One example was Soviet domination in Angola, a mineral rich country that remained desperately poor. Another was South Africa, where the racist minority government trumpeted its staunch anti-communism, discouraging the U.S. and its allies from challenging the apartheid system. It seems likely that global inequalities were enhanced as a result of the Cold War. Much time was lost in the race to development.

Following the end of the Cold War in 1989, the Soviet Union broke up into more than a dozen new states, and eastern European states abandoned their Moscow-loyal communist governments. The world economy was once again integrated, as it had been in the late nineteenth century, into a single international system dominated economically by market capitalism. Even China took an increasingly active role in world trade. The dominant nation in the system was now the U.S., but its power did not go unchallenged. The economic and political influence of Europe grew as nations there formed the European Union. Economic growth in China and India gave those countries new political clout, and the new Russian Federation, smaller than the Soviet empire but still in possession of a nuclear arsenal and huge oil reserves, could not be ignored.

Sovereignty and Rights

Another major political focus of this era was decolonization. Independence movements sprang up around the globe, and European empires crumbled one after another. Although several colonies (especially in Southeast Asia and Africa) won their freedom through constitutional change backed by vigorous political action and protest, others including Algeria, Vietnam, Afghanistan, and the Portuguese colonies in Africa, fought prolonged and bloody revolutionary wars against their colonial masters.

The last half of the twentieth century witnessed not only the triumph of anti-colonial nationalism all across the globe, but also the assertion of global human rights, as embodied in the United Nations Universal Declaration of Human Rights of 1948. The UN established a Commission on Human Rights based in Geneva, together with the High Commissioner for Human Rights. On March 15, 2006, the United Nations Human Rights Council was established as a further demonstration of the seriousness of the UN's commitment to global human rights. The efforts of the UN over the past half century have led to the increasing recognition of the existence of global human rights as a standard by which to measure national and local practices.

The UN Declaration of Human Rights of 1948 had important consequences across the entire spectrum of rights. For example, the assertion of rights of children dates to a 1923 League of Nations declaration. The 1989 UN Declaration of the Rights of the Child strongly supported children's rights and established a number of international bodies charged with their enforcement. Finally, against the background of increasing evidence of slavery and human trafficking, the world has been more alert to the fact that bonded servitude, believed to have been formally abolished in the nineteenth century, was spreading once again. Various agencies, including UNESCO, the International Labor Organization, and Anti-Slavery International have endeavored to document slavery and to enforce laws against it around the world.

The Passing of Peasantries

Big Era Nine represented the near destruction of the world's rural peasantry. For thousands of years, most people in the world had been peasants farming small areas of land. Following the Industrial Revolution, however, more and more peasants become wage earners. They either stayed in rural areas to work for commercial farmers, or they left for the major towns in search of wage work. The decisive changes occurred in this era when peasants came to represent a minority of the world's population. Between 1950 and 2000, the number of people living in cities rose from about 30 percent to over 50 percent. In Japan, the number of farmers fell from over 50 percent of the population in 1950 to less than 10 percent in 1985. In Colombia, Brazil, and Mexico, the percentage of farmers fell by half within just twenty years. By the

Students at the American University of Sharjah in the United Arab Emirates. This co-educational university, founded in 1997, follows an American model of higher education.

late 1980s, peasants remained a majority of the population only in Africa south of the Sahara, South and Southeast Asia, and China. Even in those regions, the proportion of rural farmers fell rapidly. The "death of the peasantry" meant the end of a way of life that had shaped the experiences of most humans since the agricultural revolution 10,000 years earlier.

Women's Rights

Women have made major gains in Big Era Nine in the long march for rights and equality. A major benchmark was the 1948 United Nations Convention on Human Rights, which declared "the equal rights of men and women." A UN Commission on Women's Rights has held regular conferences since its foundation in 1946. In 1979, the Convention on the Elimination of All Forms of Discrimination against Women was enacted. A Convention on the Elimination of All Forms of Discrimination against Women came into effect in 1981. Women now possess the right to vote in most countries in the world. With some exceptions, their right to own property is also widely recognized, though the disinheritance of women is still practiced in many peasant societies. Finally, women have had their reproductive rights recognized, a process in which the World Health Organization has played an important role even if they are not always able to exercise those rights in many societies. From the vantage point of the early twenty-first century, advances for women in Big Era Nine were impressive compared to any earlier era, but universal rights and equality are still far from full realization.

HUMANS AND IDEAS

The relationship between humans and ideas was transformed in previously unimaginable ways during this era. The advent of universal primary schooling, the modern telecommunications media and the unprecedented movements of people and ideas around the planet linked the world's peoples more closely, even while they reinforced differences between and among them. As a consequence, modern science, religion, and popular culture have all acquired an unprecedented ability to influence our lives.

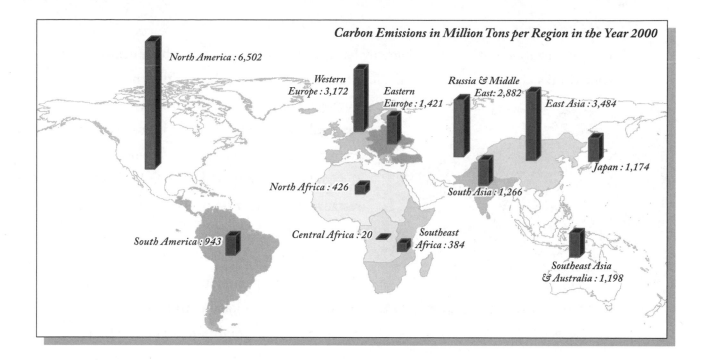

Carbon Emissions in Million Tons per Region in the Year 2000

North America : 6,502

Western Europe : 3,172

Eastern Europe : 1,421

Russia & Middle East: 2,882

East Asia : 3,484

Japan : 1,174

North Africa : 426

South Asia : 1,266

South America : 943

Central Africa : 20

Southeast Africa : 384

Southeast Asia & Australia : 1,198

Environmental Consciousness

A major arena of increased global consciousness since 1950 has been the natural and physical environment. As people have become exposed to the increasingly convincing scientific data supporting the idea of global warming, they have sought to protect natural resources and ecosystems. Today large and diverse numbers of national and international environmentalist organizations seek to encourage public awareness and action around environmental issues. Cumulatively these have generated a global conversation out of which some important institutions have emerged. One sign of this was the United Nations Conference on Environment and Development in 1992. As more people become aware of the interconnected strands that tie together the local and the global, an environmental consciousness has begun to grow.

There have been some notable successes in the campaigns to protect the environment. They are often initiated by local communities and aimed at conserving local resources such as fresh water forests. On occasion, wealthier and poorer regions have cooperated successfully to deal with environmental problems that affect the entire world. In the 1980s, for example, it became clear that the release of CFC chemicals used mainly in refrigeration threatened to break down the thin ozone layer that shields the earth from the sun's ultra-violet radiation. In 1987, an international agreement limited the production and use of CFCs, and it seems that the ozone layer may be repairing itself as a result. New energy technologies, such as wind power and hydrogen fuel cells, may eventually help reduce our dependence on fossil fuels.

Global Culture

The globalization of the world economy has transformed the way in which nearly everyone thinks about the world. At the level of popular culture, the world is more

homogenous because styles, tastes, and material goods from the more industrialized countries have spread to the rest. For example, the McDonald's chain of fast-food restaurants, which first opened in the U.S. in 1955, now has thousands of outlets throughout the world, selling variations on the same basic menu. Clothing manufacturers create styles for a global market. Popular music in a myriad of different languages and styles attracts audiences around the world. Similarly, major movies are now filmed with

A Starbucks coffee shop in the Chinese city of Xian. Why do you think an American franchise like Starbucks might be popular with some Chinese?

global audiences in mind, not just national ones. In much of the world, cultural change reflects a complex synthesis of the traditional and the modern, the local and the Western. Little of this could have been predicted before 1950.

Marxism and Neo-Liberalism

The rise of neo-liberal thought and the decline of Marxism are two other major developments of the period. The Marxist intellectual tradition presented a powerful intellectual critique of capitalism in the Cold War era. At its apex in the 1970s, that tradition inspired hundreds of thousands of intellectuals, artists, and political activists in Europe, Asia, Africa, and the Americas. With the fall of the Soviet Union and the increasing complexity of the capitalist world economy, Marxism was widely discredited as a belief system. Neo-liberalism, which preached the inevitable triumph of market forces, seemed to sweep all before it. At the end of the twenty-first century's first decade, however, the broad claims made by neo-liberal economists and politicians fell into question once again as the world plunged into a severe recession.

Religion and Science

As people throughout the world encountered one another's beliefs and values, the deepest ideas about the meaning of life have been challenged. All religions have rethought their relationships to other religions and to the secular and scientific traditions of the twentieth century. Many small, localized belief systems have died out. Major religions have also been transformed. For example, Christian music today owes a huge debt to African and African American musical traditions. Increased literacy and mass communication have helped some faiths to expand to new areas and to generate renewed commitments among their faithful. Modern media have enhanced the Pope's authority and prestige among Roman Catholics, and the pilgrimage to Mecca is now accessible to millions of Muslims, who fly to the sacred sites in Saudi Arabia from around the world.

But even as religion plays a large role in our world, so too does science. Beginning in Big Era Seven, modern science presented a formidable challenge to religious faith. The prestige of modern science derives from its universality. For all its achievements, however, science remains a rapidly evolving tradition. In Big Era Nine, fundamental new ideas, or "paradigms," emerged in several crucial disciplines, including cosmology, nuclear physics, biology, and geology. In cosmology, the "Big Bang Theory" provided an explanation of the origins of the universe. Physicists have gained deep understanding of the nature of sub-atomic particles. Biologists now grasp the role of DNA in evolutionary change. In geology, the theory of plate tectonics has provided a platform for new understanding of the development and evolution of life. As a result, scientific explanations of long-term cosmological, geological, and biological change have become increasingly well established.

> As people throughout the world encountered one another's beliefs and values, the deepest ideas about the meaning of life have been challenged.

The successes of science have also led to new problems. The biotechnological revolution gave scientists the ability to manipulate genes and, in principle, to clone animals, including human beings. Should such techniques be used? What might the consequences be? Should humans tinker with life and death in such fundamental ways? Similarly, the spectacular power humans now have over the environment poses new challenges. Should we restrain our consumption to save the environment, even if this means reducing living standards in wealthier countries and slowing, rather than speeding up, the development of poorer countries? Is it legitimate for any country to arm itself with nuclear weapons whose release would spell disaster for everyone?

Big Era Nine has been an era of staggering change and has left us with more questions than answers. Perhaps the most important question is whether or not humans will succeed at managing a global system that, as the twenty-first century moves ahead, is both complex and fragile.

CHAPTER 9 STUDY QUESTIONS

1. What relationships of cause and effect do you think might exist between global population growth, increasing demands for energy, and environmental change, including global warming? How could environmental degradation around the world be reversed if population and energy demands continue to grow?

2. How would you account for agricultural production increasing almost threefold in Big Era Nine, while the number of farmers has declined fivefold? Why do you think the percentage of the world's farming population declined so much in the twentieth century?

3. Do you think that in the past half century, the world has become increasingly "Americanized"? What are some examples of cultural Americanization? What are some examples of Americans adopting cultural ideas and practices from other parts of the world? What examples of foreign influences on your own life might you describe?

4. Do you think it is likely or not likely that nation-states will decline in importance in the coming century and international organizations such as the World Bank, Non-Governmental Organizations (NGOs), multinational corporations, and professional associations will become more important? Explain your position.

5. How would you explain growing concern in Big Era Nine for universal human rights, such as independence from imperial domination, equality for women, protection of children, and freedom from enslavement? Why were people less concerned about these issues before the twentieth century? Why did so many European imperial colonies gain independence during Big Era Nine?

Reflecting on the Past, Thinking about the Future

Historians spend a lot of time thinking about the past. Should they also ponder the future? World History for Us All explores the past at some very large scales. By doing so, it shows the existence of some very large trends. Some trends are so large that they will surely persist far into the future. This makes it tempting to try to peek into the future as well as the past, for we know that these trends will not change overnight. What might happen to humanity and its earthly environment in Big Era Ten or beyond? The very large trends should give us some clues.

But how do you think about the future? Here are some basic principles of futurology.

First Principle:
The Future Really Is Unpredictable

It is not just that we do not know enough. In the nineteenth century, many physicists, for example, Pierre-Simon, the Marquis de Laplace (1749–1827), believed that if we knew enough about the motion and energy of every particle in the universe, we could predict the future with perfect accuracy. In the twentieth century, quantum physics has shown that this is not true. It is impossible, even in theory, to determine with perfect accuracy the position and motion of subatomic particles.

Werner Heisenberg was known for his "uncertainty principle," a key discovery in the early development of quantum theory.

This means that there is always a bit of wiggle room in the way physical processes work. That is, there is always an element of what quantum physicists call "indeterminacy." The future is not completely predictable.

Does this mean there is no point in thinking about the future? No. There are important factors that increase the chances of some of our predictions about the future being right. We can and indeed must try to make predictions, even though we know they can never be perfect.

Second Principle: We Can Make Some Reasonably Accurate Predictions

Some processes and events are indeed unpredictable, because they are caused by sudden, unexpected changes. On June 28, 1914, Gavrilo Princip, a Bosnian Serb, assassinated the Archduke Francis Ferdinand, the heir to the Austrian throne. This event triggered World War I, but it was completely unpredictable. Princip might have failed to get close enough to his target, his gunshot might have missed, he might have gotten cold feet at the last minute. Many things could have changed the course of events that day.

Some processes, however, reflect large trends that are not so unpredictable. They can be detected by historians and may have enough momentum to persist some way into the future. For example, historians have argued that the alliance system created in the years before World War I made a war extremely likely, even if no one could predict the event that would precipitate it. Another example is population growth. It is impossible to predict each birth or death, but it is possible to determine average birth and death rates with great accuracy. And, using these statistics, specialists in population growth can predict with considerable confidence how large populations will be in the future. So, if you want to predict, the first thing to do is to be clear about the type of process you are discussing, and how predictable it is. Specialists in prediction—and you can find them at race tracks and on stock exchanges aiming to make money—begin by trying to be clear about the degree of predictability of the processes they are studying. They calculate the odds and study the form.

Third Principle: All Prediction Is a Percentage Game

Because of our first rule, specialists in prediction also know that, however good their information, they are playing a percentage game. They can never guarantee the accuracy of any particular prediction. The best that can be hoped for is to raise the percentage of correct predictions they make by carefully studying the main trends. Predictions that have failed are a reminder of the pitfalls of forecasting. Failed predictions include one in 1966 claiming that within a few decades both communicable diseases and heart disease would be wiped out. Another prediction that same year asserted that within a few decades only 10 percent of the world's population would work while the rest would be paid to be idle. Nevertheless, professional forecasters know that if you take enough care, you can increase the number of correct predictions you make. And they know that you can make money just be improving the percentage of correct prognostications. So predicting is a serious business.

Fourth Principle: Despite the Limits of Prediction, We Cannot Avoid It

In fact, prediction is something we have to do all the time. All living creatures have to predict. Every time you cross a busy road you make a prediction about the speed of

cars moving towards you. And you had better get this prediction right. If you get it wrong, the results could be unpleasant. Similarly, gazelles have to predict where they are likely to encounter lions or tigers. In fact, those gazelles that are bad at predicting danger are unlikely to live long. They will therefore have fewer offspring. This means that, over time, the skills of prediction get built into the DNA of all gazelles. Prediction is an essential feature of life in general.

> **We need to focus mainly on the large, slow-moving trends because these are the ones where the odds favor prediction. We can study these long trends over centuries, decades, or years and make some quite powerful forecasts.**

Why should historians refuse to attempt prediction? Is it not rather important to have some idea of whether the world economy is going to keep growing? Or how climate change might affect our neighborhood or country? How, then, can we apply the basic principles of futurology to the future of our world?

Study the Large, Slow Trends

We need to focus mainly on the large, slow-moving trends because these are the ones where the odds favor prediction. We can study these long trends over centuries, decades, or years and make some quite powerful forecasts. This is because large trends are a bit like the motion of an aircraft carrier. You cannot just slam on the brakes and expect an aircraft carrier to stop. It has such momentum that it will keep moving for a long time after the brakes have been applied. Here are some large trends which have a similar momentum. They therefore allow us to make some reasonably confident predictions:

- Population Growth. Unlike prices on the stock exchange, rates of population growth do not change significantly from day to day. They depend on large-scale patterns of health, attitudes about the family, and reasonably stable cultural values. Demographers have noted the colossal population increases of recent centuries but also a significant slowing down of growth rates in recent decades. These large trends give demographers confidence that they can roughly predict what the global population will be fifty years from now. Current estimates suggest in about that time span the world's population will reach between 9 and 12 billion and population growth will slow to zero. Such estimates are immensely important because they are used by governments and international agencies to plan their policies and investments.

- Energy and Resource Consumption. One of the strongest predictions we can make about the coming fifty years is that consumption of energy and resources will increase. We know this because growth rates are high in developed countries such as the USA, and they are rapidly catching up in some less developed countries such as China and India. With populations much larger in those developing economies, these changes guarantee rapid increases in consumption of energy and resources. In some areas, such as fisheries and land use, we seem to be close to global limits in resource use. Consequently, predictions about future consumption have vast implications for the way that economies plan their future.

- Scientific Innovation. Rates of scientific advance have increased for the best part of two centuries. Innovation rates are now increasing more rapidly than ever before, notably in big developing economies such as China and India. We cannot predict what innovations will pop up, but it is a good bet that the rate of innovation will remain swift over the next few decades. This is surely good news. It holds out the possibility that we will find technological fixes to old problems,

The Angel of the North. This colossal steel sculpture stands sixty-five feet above a hill in Gateshead, England. Erected in 1998, it has become one of the most recognizable pieces of monumental public art in the world. According to Antony Gormley, its creator, it functions in part "to grasp hold of the future, expressing our transition from the industrial to the information age."

including, perhaps, new ways of generating energy. But there might also be bad news. After all, scientists have developed nuclear weapons as well as antibiotics.

Do Not Overreach!

We must avoid making confident predictions where we cannot find large, relatively stable trends. Any prediction about where human society will be more than 200 years into the future probably does not mean much. The number of possibilities multiply out of control. For example, will there be a nuclear war? Will there be a global disease pandemic? Even the most powerful trends will have faded by then.

Even Some Very Remote Trends Can Be Predicted

Curiously, despite the difficulties of prediction, there are some large trends that allow us to make reasonable predictions about the very distant future: the future of the earth, for instance, or even the future of the universe.

- The future of the earth's surface. We can measure quite precisely the movement of tectonic plates, so geologists can be sure that in the next 50–100 million years the Atlantic will get wider, and the Pacific will get smaller, Australia will move closer to California, and Los Angeles will slide towards San Francisco.

- The future of the earth. We know roughly how long stars of a given size will live, so we can predict with some confidence that our sun will die in about 4 billion years. Before that happens, it will swell up and incorporate the inner planets, including our earth. Everything on those inner planets will be fried!

- The future of the universe. The key question here is whether or not the universe will keep expanding. Gravity tends to counteract the force of expansion, so if there is enough material in the universe, the expansion may be reined in completely. The universe may then start to shrink. Perhaps, eventually, it will shrink to nothingness, and the whole process will start over again! In the late 1990s, however, it was discovered that the rate of the universe's expansion is actually increasing. This suggests that an eventual collapse is unlikely. On the contrary, at present it looks as if the universe will expand, faster and faster, for ever and ever. As it does so, matter and energy will be dissipated over such vast spaces that nothing much will happen. The universe will become more and more boring. Born as we are just 13.7 billion years after the Big Bang, that is, in the youth of our universe, it seems that we live in interesting times!

We have seen that prediction is difficult. So is it worth the effort? Yes! As we have seen, we have to predict because every action we take depends on predictions about potential results. In any case, predictions about the next few generations matter greatly because today's forecasts will shape current policy. In that way, they will help determine the future, for better or worse! Predictions about the remote future have less immediate consequences for us, but they can help us think about our place within the universe. Historians, particularly world historians, should take futurology seriously.

EPILOGUE STUDY QUESTIONS

1. Why should we try to predict the future? How might humankind benefit from doing this?

2. Why do you think long-term trends are sometimes easier to predict than short term trends?

3. Taking into account the information in Chapter 9 and the forecasts in the Epilogue, are you mainly pessimistic or mainly optimistic about humankind's future in the coming century? Explain your view.

END NOTES

1 Patrick Manning, "The Problem of Interactions in World History," *American Historical Review* 101 (June 1996): 772.

2 David Christian, *Maps of Time: An Introduction to Big History* (Berkeley: University of California Press, 2004), 8.

3 Peter Lee, "Putting Principles into Practice: Understanding History," *How Students Learn: History in the Classroom: Committee on How People Learn, A Targeted Report for Teachers*, ed. Suzanne Donovan and John D. Bransford (Washington, DC: National Academies Press, 2005), 65, 68, 69.

4 Michael Geyer and Charles Bright, "World History in a Global Age," *American Historical Review* 100 (Oct. 1995): 1042.

5 *Bible: King James Version*, Gen 1: 3-5.

6 Andrew Bosworth, "World Cities and World Economic Cycles," in Stephen K. Sanderson, ed. *Civilizations and World Systems* (Walnut Creek, CA: Altamira Press, 1995), 216.

7 Data adapted from Rein Taagepera, "Size and Duration of Empires: Systematics of Size," *Social Science Research* 7 (1978): 108-127.

8 Data adapted from Massimo Livi-Bacci, *A Concise History of World Population* (Cambridge, MA: Blackwell, 1992), 31.

9 Data adapted from Rein Taagepera, "Size and Duration of Empires: Systematics of Size," *Social Science Research* 7 (1978): 108-127.

10 Christian, *Maps of Time*, 344-45.

11 Angus Maddison, *World Economy: A Millennial Perspective* (Paris: Organization for Economic Co-operation and Development, 2001), 241.

12 J. R. McNeill, *Something New under the Sun: An Environmental History of the Twentieth-Century World* (New York: Norton, 2000), 283.

13 Maddison, *World Economy*, 262.

14 Maddison, *World Economy*, 262.

15 McNeill, *Something New under the Sun*, 311.

16 McNeill, *Something New under the Sun*, 132.

17 J. R. McNeill and William H. McNeill, *The Human Web: A Bird's Eye View of World History* (New York: Norton, 2003), 316.

PICTURE CREDITS

Introduction

- "Father Time." Illustration. 1980. *Men: A Pictorial Archive from Nineteenth-Century Sources*. Mineola, NY: Dover Publications, Inc.

- "Children reading." Illustration. 1978. *Children: A Pictorial Archive from Nineteenth-Century Sources*. Mineola, NY: Dover Publications, Inc.

- "Marmite – Two Editions." Photograph. 2007. *Wikimedia Commons*, http://commons.wikimedia.org/wiki/File:Marmite-Two_editions.JPG (accessed April 2, 2012).

Chapter 1

- "The Creation of Adam." Illustration. 1980. *Men: A Pictorial Archive from Nineteenth-Century Sources*. Mineola, NY: Dover Publications, Inc.

- "Milky Way IR Spitzer." Photograph. 2006. *NASA Jet Propulsion Laboratory California Institute of Technology*, http://www.spitzer.caltech.edu/Images/1540-ssc2006-02a-A-Cauldron-of-Stars-at-the-Galaxy-s-Center (accessed April 2, 2012).

- "Pioneer plaque." Digital Image. 2006. *NASA. Wikimedia Commons*, http://commons.wikimedia.org/wiki/File:PPlaqueLarge.png (accessed April 2, 2012).

- "Hartmannella vermiformis." Digital Image. 2009. *Wikimedia Commons*, http://commons.wikimedia.org/wiki/File:Hartmannella_vermiformis.jpg (accessed April 2, 2012).

- "Homo erectus skull—Naturmuseum Freiburg." Photograph. 2011. *Wikimedia Commons*, http://commons.wikimedia.org/wiki/File:Homo_erectus_skull_-_Naturmuseum_Freiburg_-_DSC06767.jpg (accessed April 2, 2012).

- Cohen, Kathleen. "Biface hand axes." Photograph. ca. 150,000–40,000 BP. *World Images*, http://worldImages.sjsu.edu/Obj9466?sid=3926&x=2273721 (accessed April 2, 2012).

Chapter 2

- Cohen, Kathleen. "Bone fish hooks." Photograph. ca. 25,000–15,000 BP. *World Images*, http://worldImages.sjsu.edu/Obj9472?sid=42537&x=11895895 (accessed April 2, 2012).

- Cohen, Kathleen. "Paleolithic dwelling. Mammoth bones." Photograph. ca. 16,000–10,000 BP. *World Images*, http://worldImages.sjsu.edu/Obj9455?sid=42537&x=11900147 (accessed April 2, 2012).

- Cohen, Kathleen. "Hall of the Bulls." Photograph. 15,000–10,000 BP. *World Images*, http://worldImages.sjsu.edu/Obj55699?sid=8978&x=10286814 (accessed April 2, 2012).

- "Venus von Willendorf." Photograph. 2011. *Wikimedia Commons*, http://commons.wikimedia.org/wiki/File:Venus_von_Willendorf_01.png (accessed April 2, 2012).

Chapter 3

- "British Museum Copper Bull." Photograph. 2010. *Wikimedia Commons*, http://commons.wikimedia.org/wiki/File:British_Museum_Copper_Bull.JPG (accessed April 2, 2012).

Chapter 4

- "British Museum Room 10 cuneiform." Photograph. 2011. *Wikimedia Commons*, http://commons.wikimedia.org/wiki/File:British_Museum_Room_10_cuneiform.jpg (accessed April 2, 2012).

- "Roman road of Santa Agueda." Photograph. 2006. *Wikimedia Commons*, http://commons.wikimedia.org/wiki/File:Roman_road_of_Santa_Agueda_.jpg (accessed April 2, 2012).

Chapter 5

- Livi-Bacci, Massimo. "Global Population Trend (in millions)." Adapted from *A Concise History of World Population* (Cambridge, MA: Blackwell, 1992), 31.

- "Arabisches Astrolabium." Photograph. 2010. *Wikimedia Commons*, http://commons.wikimedia.org/wiki/File:GNM_-_Arabisches_Astrolabium.jpg (accessed April 2, 2012).

- "Three estates of medieval society." Illustration. 2011. *Wikimedia Commons*, http://commons.wikimedia.org/wiki/File:Three-estates-prognosticatio-lichtenberger-mainz-1492.jpg (accessed April 2, 2012).

- Dunn, Ross. "Great Zimbabwe Enclosure Wall." Photograph.

- Dunn, Ross. "Durham Chapel." Photograph.

- Dunn, Ross. "Great Buddha carving." Photograph.

- Dunn, Ross. "Pure Light Dharani Sutra." Photograph.

- Dunn, Ross. "Attarin College." Photograph.

- Dunn, Ross. "Old Court of Corpus Christi College." Photograph.

Chapter 6

- Biard, Auguste François. "The Slave Trade." Painting. 1840. *Wikimedia Commons*, http://commons.wikimedia.org/wiki/File:The_Slave_Trade_by_Auguste_Francois_Biard.jpg (accessed April 2, 2012).

- Dunn, Ross. "Lombard cannon." Photograph.

- "Tsar cannon." Photograph. 2009. *Wikimedia Commons*, http://commons.wikimedia.org/wiki/File:Tsar_Cannon.JPG (accessed April 2, 2012).

- Cohen, Kathleen. "Sofonisba Anguissola." Painting. 1554. *World Images*, http://worldImages.sjsu.edu/Obj12920?sid=8978&x=3971914 (accessed April 2, 2012).

- "Gutenberg press." Photograph. 2011. *Wikimedia Commons*, http://commons.wikimedia.org/wiki/File:PrintMus_038.jpg (accessed April 2, 2012).

- Cohen, Kathleen. "Minaret from Djinguareben Mosque." Photograph. 1355. *World Images*, http://worldImages.sjsu.edu/Obj83043?sid=8978&x=3972824 (accessed April 2, 2012).

Chapter 7

- Dunn, Ross. "Coal mine." Photograph.

- "Leaving old England for America." Illustration. 1870. Library of Congress Prints and Photographs Online Catalog. http://www.loc.gov/pictures/item/97512198/ (accessed April 2, 2012).

- Davis, Mike. "Victims of famine." Photograph.

- Duncan, Edward. "Destroying Chinese war junks." Painting. 1843. *Wikimedia Commons*, http://commons.wikimedia.org/wiki/File:Destroying_Chinese_war_junks,_by_E._Duncan_(1843).jpg (accessed April 2, 2012).

- Dunn, Ross. Artist unknown. "Battle of Adowa." Painting.

- Vilimek, Jan. "Charles Darwin." Illustration. 1889. *Wikimedia Commons*, http://commons.wikimedia.org/wiki/File:Charles_Darwin_-_Jan_Vilímek.jpg (accessed April 2, 2012).

- Mayall, John. "Karl Marx." Photograph. 1875. *Wikimedia Commons*, http://commons.wikimedia.org/wiki/File:Karl_Marx_001.jpg (accessed April 2, 2012).

Chapter 8

- McNeill, J. R. "Change in Percent of Population Living in Cities." Adapted from table in *Something New Under the Sun: An Environmental History of the Twentieth-Century World* (New York: Norton, 2000), 283.

- Monet, Claude. "The Sun Shining Through the Fog." Painting. 1904. *Wikimedia Commons*, http://commons.wikimedia.org/wiki/File:Claude_Monet_015.jpg (accessed April 2, 2012).

- "German stormtroops training Sedan May 1917." Photograph. 1917. *Wikimedia Commons*, http://commons.wikimedia.org/wiki/File:German_stormtroops_training_Sedan_May_1917_3.jpg (accessed April 2, 2012).

- "Vladimir Ilyich Lenin." Photograph. ca. 1920. *Soyuzfoto Soviet News Agency*. *Wikimedia Commons*, http://commons.wikimedia.org/wiki/File:Lenin_CL.jpg (accessed April 2, 2012).

- "Mustafa Kemal Ataturk." Photograph. ca. 1920. *Images Ataturk collection of the Republic of Turkey Ministry of National Education. Wikimedia Commons,* http://commons.wikimedia.org/wiki/File:Ataturk-1930-amongpublic.jpg (accessed April 2, 2012).

- "Buchenwald Survivor Identifies Guard." Photograph. 1945. *Wikimedia Commons,* http://commons.wikimedia.org/wiki/File:Buchenwald_Survivor_Identifies_Guard_2.jpg (accessed April 2, 2012).

- "Franklin D. Roosevelt having a fireside chat in Washington, D.C." Photograph. 1935. *U.S. National Archives and Records Administration. Wikimedia Commons,* http://commons.wikimedia.org/w/index.php?title=File:Franklin_D._Roosevelt_having_a_fireside_chat_in_Washington,_D.C_-_NARA_-_196760.tif&page=1 (accessed April 2, 2012).

Chapter 9

- "Titan I ICBM." Photograph. 1959. *U.S. Air Force. Wikimedia Commons,* http://commons.wikimedia.org/wiki/File:Titan_I_ICBM.jpg (accessed April 2, 2012).

- Dunn, Ross. "Students at the American University of Sharjah." Photograph.

- Dunn, Ross. "Chinese Starbucks." Photograph.

Epilogue

- "Werner Heisenberg in front of the Urfeld house." Photograph. *University of New Hampshire,* http://werner-heisenberg.unh.edu/ (accessed April 2, 2012).

- Dunn, Ross. "Angel of the North." Photograph.

FOR FURTHER READING

Bain, Robert. "'They Thought the World Was Flat?' Principles in Teaching High School History," in *How Students Learn: History, Math and Science in the Classroom.* M. Suzanne Donovan and John D. Bransford, eds. Washington: National Academy Press, 2005.

Bentley, Jerry H. *Shapes of World History in Twentieth-Century Scholarship.* Essays on Global and Comparative History. Edited by Michael Adas. Washington, D.C.: American Historical Association, 1996.

————, ed. *The Oxford Handbook of World History.* Oxford: Oxford UP, 2011.

Brown, Cynthia Stokes. *Big History: From the Big Bang to the Present.* New York: The New Press, 2007.

Christian, David. *This Fleeting World: A Short History of Humanity.* Great Barrington, MA: Berkshire Publishing, 2008.

————, *Maps of Time: An Introduction to Big History.* Berkeley: University of California Press, 2004.

Cohen, Sharon. *AP World History: Teacher's Guide.* New York: College Board, 2007.

Crossley, Pamela Kyle. *What Is Global History?* Malden, MA: Polity, 2008.

Dunn, Ross E., ed. *The New World History: A Teacher's Companion.* Boston: Bedford St. Martins, 2000.

————. "The Two World Histories." *Social Education* 72 (Sept. 2008): 257-263.

Dunn, Ross E. and David Vigilante, eds. *Bring History Alive: A Sourcebook for Teaching World History.* Los Angeles: National Center for History in the Schools, UCLA, 1996.

Hodgson, Marshall G. S. *Rethinking World History: Essays on Europe, Islam, and World History.* Edited by Edmund Burke III. Cambridge: Cambridge UP, 1993.

Hopkins, A. G., ed. *Global History: Interactions between the Universal and the Local.* New York: Palgrave, 2006.

Hughes-Warrington, Marnie, ed. *World Histories.* New York: Palgrave Macmillan, 2005.

Manning, Patrick. *Navigating World History: Historians Create a Global Past.* New York: Palgrave Macmillan, 2003.

————, ed. *World History: Global and Local Interactions.* Princeton: Markus Wiener, 2005.

Pomper, Philip, Richard H. Elphick, and Richard T. Vann, eds. *World History: Ideologies, Structures, and Identities.* Malden, MA: Blackwell, 1998.

Roupp, Heidi, ed. *Teaching World History: A Resource Book.* Armonk, N.Y.: M. E. Sharpe, 1997.

Spier, Fred. *Big History and the Future of Humanity*. Malden, MA: Wiley-Blackwell, 2011.

"The New World History: How Can We Bring Our Students' World into the Classroom?" *Social Studies Review* 49 (Spring/Summer 2010).

Index